# MONTEZUMA'S SERPENT

## *And Other True Supernatural Tales of the Southwest*

**Brad Steiger & Sherry Hansen-Steiger**

**Paragon House**
**New York**

Montezuma's Serpent
And Other True Supernatural Tales
of the Southwest
Brad Steiger and Sherry Hansen-Steiger

Paragon House
New York
First edition, 1992

Published in the United States by
Paragon House
90 Fifth Avenue
New York, N.Y. 10011

Library of Congress Cataloging-in-Publishing data

Steiger, Brad.
    Montezuma's serpent and other true supernatural tales of the
Southwest / Brad Steiger and Sherry Hansen-Steiger.
        p.  cm.
        ISBN 1-55778-474-4
        1. Tales—Southwest, New.  2. Supernatural.  3. Indians of
North America—Southwest, New—Legends.  I. Steiger, Sherry
Hansen.  II. Title.
GR108.5.S74  1992
398.25—dc20                                        92-8421
                                                       CIP

Manufactured in the United States of America

# Contents

✲

# PREFACE

The lure of the mystical Southwest has never been stronger than it is today. National television programs devote lengthy features to the mystery of the Sedona vortexes, evidence of crashed UFOs in New Mexico, the enigma of massive Bigfoot creatures in California, the manifestation of Indian ghosts in Texas, and unclaimed Spanish gold with deadly curses in Arizona.

For several decades we have been collecting tales of the strange, the unusual, and the supernatural; and we have written numerous books that explore the far reaches of the Unknown. We could not help noticing in our files how many dramatic stories of strange disappearances, spook lights, impossible fossils, mysterious mummies, unidentified prehistoric ruins, and downright spine-tingling accounts of haunted houses have taken place in the mountains, deserts, and canyons of the American Southwest. It thus seemed a natural thing to write a book that would contain some of the eeriest supernatural tales of the Southwest. And it seemed proper to kick off the collection with the legend of the giant serpent of Montezuma, the great culture-bearer of the Southwest.

The operative word in this book's title is *tales*. We do not offer you a learned thesis on folklore—nor do we suggest that all of these stories can be proved under scientific analysis. We have documented them to the best of our ability whenever we are recount-

ing a tale concerning actual personages and events. Otherwise we are simply repeating them in the manner in which they were shared with us. As with so many accounts of ghostly occurrences, prophetic visions, and marvelous miracles, truth and reality may be in the mind and the eye of the beholder.

The characters in these tales are a mixed lot, and the range of viewpoints and biases presented here fairly mirrors humankind. Of course, within each person, family, nation, or ethnic group are elements of both good and evil. Not all Indians were scalpers and bloodthirsty savages; nor all settlers and trappers, gunfighters and murderers. Not all Spaniards were gold-crazed treasure-hunters and bandits any more than all Indians were wise shamans or all whites greed-driven carpetbaggers.

While some of the stories in this book may seem to have conflicting philosophies, the reader should bear in mind their wholistic messages. Among our Native American friends and in the teachings of the Medicine Priests such as Rolling Thunder, Twylah, Sun Bear, and Grandfather David, there is a common thread about a special and unique relationship with nature, the sacredness and inter-relatedness of all things, the ethics of personal responsibility, and the urgency of prophecies that must now be shared.

In spite of their common thread, however, they may differ on methods, techniques, or details, but in reality those differences do not alter the central message and core of what they teach and represent. That essential core deals always with the polarities of life—and the process of finding and maintaining the balance in between. It is the variety of color and patterns in these tales of the Southwest that transforms the individual threads into a priceless tapestry woven together with the binding thread of truth.

Throughout we have assumed the time-honored mantle of the storyteller. This is a book to enjoy, to puzzle over, to contemplate. It is entirely up to readers to accept those stories they wish to accept as accurate accounts and the gospel truth and those tales they wish to attribute to long nights and good whiskey.

There is nothing wrong with healthy skepticism regarding some of the tales, but don't be too quick to dismiss all of these accounts

with a contemptuous, "'tain't so." We suggest that readers simply approach these tales as mysteries. We have seldom met an intelligent, unbiased person who was not intrigued by the Unknown. As Raymond Chandler once said, "Show me a man or woman who cannot stand mysteries, and I will show you a fool; a clever fool—perhaps—but a fool just the same."

The immense fascination with the Southwestern traditions and folklore has spread not only throughout the Americas, but throughout Europe and Asia as well. Japanese clothing companies have set up terminals to buy used blue jeans—for which they pay the owner cash—because they want the cowboy look of the Southwest. Turquoise jewelry, oversized belt buckles, brightly colored clothing, Native American herbs for healing and seasoning, Southwest art, cowboy hats and boots are becoming the in-thing around the globe. Even as we write this, in February 1992, it has just been reported that salsa, a traditional Southwestern chip dip, has for the first time outsold All-American catsup!

But our fascination goes far beyond the trendy jeans, jewelry, oversized belt buckles, and bolo ties. Our focus in this book is on the folklore, the mystique, the very spiritual essence, if you will, of the Southwest. Travel the deserts at night; stand at the edge of the Grand Canyon at sunset; look out over the Pacific Ocean at dawn. You will feel an energy, an awesome sense of Oneness with the Earth Mother, a respect for the workings of nature, a passion for the unity of all people of good will that you will experience in no other place. In the Southwest it is easy to believe in the supernatural—and in second chances.

Perhaps all the world wants to relive the dream of "going West" to enliven our lives with the promise of gold, rainbows, and clear skies. Perhaps we all want a chance to start over and to learn the simpler, more natural, ways of living. The Southwest is truly a land of sunshine and blue skies, as well as a country of rich folklore and supernatural tales.

Sherry Hansen-Steiger
Brad Steiger
Cave Creek, Arizona

# CHAPTER ONE

# THE SACRED SERPENT OF MONTEZUMA

"I first saw the great serpent when I was a boy in New Mexico,"
Reuben Montoya said. "I think it was around nineteen-forty. I
was eleven years old. We lived in a village that had much talk of
witches and devils.

"I was walking with my grandfather late at night, and suddenly
we came upon this huge rattlesnake in an arroyo. It coiled itself,
and it was still taller than Grandfather. Its body was thicker than a
strong man's leg."

Reuben remembered freezing in complete terror as the gigantic
serpent bobbed its great head scant inches away from his face.
"Grandfather, too, was unable to move or to speak. But I did not
have time to worry about Grandfather. The great rattlesnake's
tongue touched the tip of my nose, and I felt my heart stop in
fright. Soon, I knew, it would bite me and kill me."

But the terrible piercing of flesh with fangs, the awful expected
injection of fiery poison never came. The huge snake weaved
before Reuben for what seemed to be an eternity, then it disappeared in a cloud of smoke that smelled something like spent shotgun shells.

"My grandfather was at last able to move, and he knelt beside
me and put his arms around me," Reuben said. "He began to
weep, but I soon learned his tears were not from thankfulness that

I had been spared death at the fangs of the monstrous snake."

"Oh, Reuben, my boy," his grandfather managed to speak between great, gasping sobs. "You were visited by the sacred serpent of Montezuma. If you had only kissed the snake's tongue, you would have been granted much wisdom and many powers not available to ordinary men."

Then, suddenly, his grandfather was angry with him. It was as though Reuben had failed a very important test and had brought disgrace upon his family. He too began to cry when his grandfather slapped his face, and he ran the rest of the way home to the security of his mother's arms.

"She explained to me then about the wonderful Montezuma, the almighty, powerful sorcerer, and his sacred serpent, a *biborón*, a monster rattlesnake," Reuben remembered. "She did not scold me for not kissing the serpent's tongue. She said that you must be certain that it is not the Devil in disguise who appears before you. She told me that the Devil will often trick vain and ambitious men by appearing as the sacred serpent.

"'You must prepare yourself and be ready if the serpent should visit you again,' she said."

According to Reuben, who now lives in Arizona and is respected as a great healer, the serpent did manifest again before him when he was a youth of twenty-two.

"I had been on a seven-day fast. I had undergone several sessions in a sweat lodge* and I had purified my body. When Montezuma's sacred serpent appeared before me, it opened its mouth wide, very wide, so that I could place my entire head between its jaws. I did so without fear, and I received the blessing of becoming a healer."

"I think that Montezuma was the reincarnation of Quetzalcoatl,

---

* The sweat lodge was used by nearly all tribes north of Mexico. It was usually a small round house made of sod or hides. Hot rocks and water were placed inside to cause steam. Special "sweats" were used for religious purposes and to purify oneself for certain rituals.

the great Aztec culture-bearer," observed Juan Two Bears, a college-educated thirty-four-year-old ranch hand of Blackfoot heritage. "He would have ruled all of the Americas had it not been for the treachery of the Spanish. Because he was such a master sorcerer, however, he was able to return in his spirit body after his death and manifest even greater power as a Light Being."

Juan went on his vision* quest in the San Francisco mountains near Flagstaff, Arizona. "When the sacred serpent called me to its cave, I went willingly. I had already prayed most of the fear out of my body, but I will always remember that huge mouth opening to receive my ultimate expression of faith and trust. I put my head inside its jaws so that I could receive great Medicine power."

No one quite remembers exactly where the old trading post was that a man named Malcolm Graves (or Reeves) ran in the White Mountains of Arizona sometime in the 1870s. According to legend, he was a cruel and perverse man who had made slaves of some Apaches who had fallen into his debt. Then, for his own amusement, that of his wife Antonia, and those men who paid him well, the trader submitted the captive Apaches and their women to systematic torture and sexual abuse. The trading post became a hellhole.

The great Apache sorcerer Patch was told of the disgrace, and he invoked the spirit of the god-man Montezuma to assist him in the delivery of his people from the awful thing that had befallen them. In answer to Patch's ten days of fasting and chanting, Montezuma sent his *biborón* to exact revenge on the evil trader and his wife Antonia.

---

* During the vision quest, the supplicants go apart by themselves to fast, to pray, to seek their spiritual guide, and to receive their special name. The personal revelatory experience received during the vision quest becomes the fundamental guiding force in any traditional Amerindian's medicine. The dogma of tribal rituals and the religious expressions of others become secondary to the guidance one receives from personal visions. The vision quest is basic to all Native American religious experience.

Once the giant rattlesnake had dispatched the two sadists, Patch placed their spirits into a nether world where they could be held until they had been purified. According to local legend, however, the ghosts of Malcolm and Antonia have made their way out of limbo on more than one occasion.

The alleged site of the old trading post has been little more than clumps of stones and bricks for many years, but there are those who have camped in the area who swear they have heard the screams of men and women in awful pain issuing from the ruins.

Around the turn of the century, a hunter and his wife reported that they had encountered a hulking, coarse man who seemed to be following them through the forested area. After a time, it began to appear that rather than following them, the brutish fellow was herding them toward a particular area.

It was early nightfall when they approached the trading post that had been the scene of so much brutality and so many evil deeds. The place had become a shambles soon after the death of Graves and his wife, and the couple had heard the stories about the post being haunted. They became even more uneasy when they saw the shimmering image of a woman standing in the doorway of the deserted store.

"She seemed to be beckoning for us to enter," the hunter stated. "Both my wife and I were becoming mesmerized by the apparition, and we felt ourselves drawn toward the old trading post against our wills."

That was when an Apache medicine man with a patch over one eye seemed to appear out of nowhere. The hunter and his wife were startled to see a gigantic rattlesnake at his side.

"Leave this place!" the elderly Apache told them.

According to the hunter's account, "We did not hesitate to take immediate heed of his warning."

In the summer of 1989, a young man of Pima Indian and Hispanic heritage from Scottsdale, Arizona, vowed that he would undertake a traditional vision quest. It was not at all difficult to

4

find an isolated area in the Superstition Mountains near Phoenix where he might be undisturbed for many days.

"On the fifth day of my quest, I had suffered through a day of 115-degree heat, and I had begun to think that maybe those old traditional Indians were a lot tougher than I was," he said. "I decided to remain there for at least that night. I had not yet received anything that I might call a true vision, but I had told so many of my friends about my intention to hold an authentic vision quest that I felt that I must stick it out as long as I could.

"Shortly after one of those fantastic Arizona sunsets, I began to sing and to pray," he continued. "I don't know how long I kept this up before I entered a very deep meditative state. I do know, with all my essence, however, that I truly did enter a separate reality. Before me, as clearly as I have ever seen anything in my life, I saw the sacred serpent of Montezuma. It was as big as an anaconda from the Amazon. It had to be at least thirty feet long."

Within a few moments, the young man remembered, the image of Montezuma appeared in his full majesty. "He was magnificent! He was dressed in multicolored robes that seemed to be woven of brilliant feathers, culled from the bright plumage of exotic birds. He stood at least seven feet tall. In one hand he held a kind of scepter. The other hand rested on the head of this enormous serpent. Montezuma told me that I must always stay on the true Medicine path and not be seduced by the false promises of materialism."

"We don't really know when it happened," our Navajo friend, the artist David Little Turtle, said, "but the historical Montezuma became somehow translated into a culture hero who is usually associated with good, with white magic. Because the entities of certain tribes maintain a duality, however, among some traditions he is also recognized as a practitioner of black magic."

David explained that the more the Roman Catholic missionaries to the area had tried to stamp out a virtual worship of Montezuma and his sacred serpent, the more they assured the acceptance of the

Aztec leader as the protector of native religion and the traditional ways. The harder the priests tried to brand Montezuma a devil, the more appealing he became to a people oppressed by the white men and their God of wrath.

"It was not long before people were healing in Montezuma's name, blessing the hunt in Montezuma's name, and growing corn in Montezuma's name," David said.

The historical Montezuma ruled the Aztec Empire from about 1503 until his death in 1520. He may have been something of a mystic, but in the folklore of the native people of the Southwest he has become the embodiment of arcane wisdom and powerful magic. His great sacred serpent appears to serve as a kind of messenger of the Medicine Brotherhood who initiates the worthy ones who seek higher paths of knowledge and loftier ideals of service.

We would be likely to assume that accounts of the sacred serpent most often occur in visionary experiences, but there are unpleasant legends of a giant reptile to which certain frightened inhabitants of Pueblo villages have offered small children to appease the wrath of an evil entity.

Cleo Jaramillo, who set down a number of folk legends of New Mexico in *Shadows of the Past*, states that many Hispanics in the area of Taos Pueblo held to the belief that the Indians of that village sheltered a divine serpent. The tale also maintained that on special feast days infants were fed to the monster rattlesnake.

In his *Commerce of the Prairies*, Josiah Gregg reported, "On one occasion I heard an honest ranchero assert, that entering Pecos very early on a winter's morning, he saw the huge trail of the reptile in the snow, as large as that of an ox being dragged."

In *Witchcraft in the Southwest*, Marc Simmons summarizes the popular New Mexican folk myth that has Montezuma being born among the Rio Grande Indians and becoming recognized as a mighty ruler and priest in the pueblo of Pecos. Possessed of unpar-

alleled supernatural powers, Montezuma took a Zuñi girl as his bride and queen, then climbed aboard a giant eagle to fly south in order to build Tenochtitlán (Mexico City), the capital of his empire.

Scholars now generally believe that the Pueblo and other tribes first learned of Montezuma through the Spanish conquistadors and their Mexican-Indian servants. The Spanish might have told their version of the conquest of the Aztecs and their emperor as a kind of object lesson to the tribes of the Southwest that they should not attempt to resist. What really took seed in the imaginations of the native tribes people, however, was the mystique of Montezuma, the wonder worker of magic. In less than a century the Aztec leader had become completely incorporated into the folklore and tradition of the Pueblo Indians. From New Mexico, stories of the feats of Montezuma spread to other tribes.

Legends grew of the sacred fire that Montezuma had kindled centuries before he left for Mexico to build the Aztec empire. If one were to find the sacred fire, he would receive immortality and unlimited magical powers.

While those of a spiritual frame of mind may have been driven to search for the everlasting fire of Montezuma that could endow its discoverer with everlasting life and illumination, those of a more material inclination became inflamed by tales of the Azetc emperor's vast storehouses of hidden wealth. Many Hispanics and Anglos began desperate searches into various dangerous mountain areas to claim Montezuma's vast treasure. Although some Indian accounts stated that the gold-seekers were struck down by lightning from the skies for daring to profane Montezuma's booty, the treasure-hunters were not dissuaded from their efforts.

In the late 1960s, a treasure-hunter claimed to have discovered Aztec glyphs etched into manmade steps in White Mountain, Utah, outside the town of Kanab. Although the treasure trove remains undiscovered, some say that these glyphs offer the first solid clues to the location of ten million dollars in gold and precious gems which Montezuma shipped north to prevent its falling into the hands of the Spanish invaders.

✛

"I know that on some level of reality Montezuma lives," a young practitioner of traditional Indian medicine told us. "And I know that the sacred serpent is a very real and important aspect of receiving heavy Medicine power."

This, according to the Cherokee traditionalist, Ray, is how he received his blessing from Montezuma's serpent:

"I had fasted for six days before I entered the Medicine circle that I had drawn in the clearing. I had an amulet that had been given to me by my teacher-Medicine priest. I offered my prayer that no negative entities would enter my circle of protection.

"I waited another day and into the night before the great serpent appeared at the edge of my circle. It towered over me. I know that it was over thirty feet long and it had to weigh well over two hundred pounds. It coiled, and its head still hovered over me. It distended its jaw so that it could encompass my skull.

"I knew what I must do, and I submitted my head to the great serpent's mouth. I stood motionless to prove my faith and my lack of fear as the massive serpentine jaws moved over my face and the long, curved fangs gently touched the back of my neck.

"And then the sacred serpent was gone. I could feel the blessing of great Medicine power flowing through me like a warm, tingling surge of electricity. I had received the great initiation from Montezuma's serpent. My life had been blessed, and I shall never be the same person that I was. I will always follow the true Medicine path of higher spirituality."

# CHAPTER TWO

# THE AWFUL REVENGE OF THE CHINDI, THE NAVAJO'S AVENGING ANGEL

**"**The very greatest of the Navajo medicine men have the ability to sing into existence a Chindi, a guardian spirit, to do their bidding," our friend Don Red Fox said. "They can send this Chindi even to faraway places to work justice on those who have wronged the medicine man or his people."

Don was a master player in two worlds. He had a Ph. D. in sociology, and was a member of the Mesquakie (Fox), a tribe that closely maintained the traditional spiritual ways of their ancestors. He was an expert on the traditions of several Native American tribes, and he had been assigned by a combined council of Plains Indians the responsiblity of seeking the return of Indian skeletons and mummies to their appropriate tribal structures for ceremonial reburials.

It was a perfect night to hold such a discussion about avenging angels, demons, and other things that go bump in the night in the high desert country of Arizona. A low wind was moaning around the pillars of our patio in Cave Creek, and we could see the full moon trying to escape from thick, dark clouds. We had enjoyed a hearty meal of chicken fajitas, refried beans, and Spanish rice, and now it was time to tell tales of ghosts, werecreatures, and the Chindi.

"You must always remember," David Little Turtle said, entering

the conversation, "that we believe that the essence of the Great Mystery, the Great Spirit, if you will, can be found in everything. We revere and have a great passion for the Earth Mother, and we traditional Indians are very much aware of our place in the web of life and our responsibility for all plant and animal life."

David, our other guest that evening, was what some tribes would call a "Meti" (pronounced may-tee), one of mixed blood. His mother was a Navajo, his father an itinerant preacher of Irish-American stock. David grew up on the Navajo reservation at Window Rock, and he traveled the world as a merchant seaman before becoming recognized as a painter of exquisite Southwestern landscapes and uniquely stylized portraits of Native American life. As a Navajo, David felt particularly qualified to talk about the Chindi, a kind of avenging angel in the tradition of his tribe.

"It is a wanton disrespect for that natural web of life that most often sets a Chindi in motion," David emphasized, reaching for another of the little cigars that he liked to smoke. "A Chindi can come alive when someone thoughtlessly violates the Earth Mother or behaves in an irresponsible manner toward plant or animal life. Sometimes, even disrespect for rocks and landscape will bring about punishment by the Chindi."

"It seems to be something like an angry nature spirit," we suggested. "Like a violated deva or a perturbed fairy or elf."

"Only in its milder manifestations," David agreed tentatively. "From what I understand of various European supernatural traditions, the Chindi is a lot like what might be referred to as a familiar spirit. But if anyone shows disrespect to any of the Earth Mother's creatures, the Chindi becomes very much like an avenging angel, and it may seek retribution."

We wanted to know what form a Chindi took to work its acts of retribution.

"It can assume any shape," David Little Turtle answered. Then he shook his head in self-correction. "More accurately stated, it can *inhabit* any living thing. Almost any traditional Navajo has at least one Chindi story to tell. He or she will tell you about driving home at night and seeing a coyote walking on its hind legs."

*"Its hind legs?"*

"Yes," Don Red Fox confirmed over the rim of his coffee cup. "That is one of the ways of knowing that an animal harbors a Chindi. The other sure way of identifying an animal so possessed is the fact that its eyes will appear dead. For example, if your headlights hit the animal's eyes and they do not reflect the light, you will know that a Chindi has inhabited the creature."

We wanted to know what would happen if one should meet such a coyote walking on its hind legs while on an evening's stroll in the desert.

"It will not necessarily harm you," David said, somewhat reassuringly.

"How the Chindi responds to you depends upon your attitude toward the Earth Mother and whether or not you have a good heart," Don interjected.

"But even if you think you have your act pretty well together," David added, "it would still be best to draw a Medicine circle around you and to say or sing a prayer for protection. It need not be a Navajo chant. Sing any prayer that you know. The important thing is your attitude."

Don Red Fox sipped at his coffee and set the cup back on its saucer. His tone was very serious as he added to his friend's admonition. "If you should have performed an act of desecration to the Earth Mother in any way or if a Chindi should have been set against you for any reason, you can only stop the energy by a Medicine circle, a powerful song, or by maintaining such a pure heart that the energy will boomerang and return to the one who set it upon you."

We had to draw the worst-case scenario: "But what if you don't know how to draw a proper Medicine circle or sing the right song? And what if you have just unknowingly violated a sacred patch of desert? How do you stop a Chindi? With a silver bullet?"

David smiled and then soberly informed us that any kind of bullet would kill the Chindi's host animal.

"But there is *no* kind of bullet that will stop a Chindi," Don said firmly.

11

"If you kill the host animal," David explained, "the Chindi will simply enter another animal. And another and another ... until it has worked its vengeance on you."

✛

The tragic account of the Navajo Long Salt family comprises the most completely documented story of the Chindi's persistence in exacting vengeance. In the case of the Long Salts, the avenging spirit pursued the family over a tormented trail of suffering that took a hundred years to complete.

The ordeal of the Long Salts began in 1825, when a man of the family became ill because of nightmares that endlessly troubled his sleep.

"It is Dawn Dancer," he told his brother. "His spirit comes to me when I sleep, and he tries to smother my spirit."

"But Dawn Dancer is dead," his brother protested. "He was our enemy for years. You killed him after a great fight. You were justified in killing him."

"But his spirit is restless." The tormented man slumped to the ground in his weakness. "I killed him before he could sing his death song. My brother, you must find a Medicine priest to rid me of Dawn Dancer's spirit—or I shall die."

As they were directed, the afflicted man's brothers sought assistance from an old, blind medicine man from the Tsegi country who, at their request, held a three-day *b'jene* (sing) over the victimized sleeper. After the last day of the ritual, the man sighed his gratitude that the restless spirit had departed and that he could now enter a healing sleep.

For part of his pay, the medicine priest asked five butchered sheep from the Long Salt family's valuable flock. But since the flock was grazing at some distance from the village, the two Long Salt men assigned the task of slaughtering the sheep decided to substitute five wild antelope in their place. After all, they assured one another, the old man was blind anyway. He wouldn't be able to tell the difference, and they would preserve five precious sheep for the family's own use.

12

The old medicine priest was escorted to his home with the honors due his position and the thanks accrued from the successful healing of the troubled member of the Long Salt family. The Long Salt elder who awarded the medicine priest the five carcasses were unaware that antelope had been substituted for the specified sheep. With the animals' heads cut off and the lower legs removed at the knees, even with their full sight they had been unable to detect the deceit the two members of their family had perpetrated.

A few weeks later, an older member of the Long Salt family died. Although some considered it strange that the elderly man had not suffered any illness before his sudden death, it was not really deemed remarkable that an aged one should pass away.

But then a robust and healthy young Long Salt fell dead for no perceptible reason. As his pregnant wife and his parents sang their songs of mourning, other family members fought a growing feeling of uneasiness. Something very wrong was occurring in their midst.

Every few weeks after the young husband's death, a member of the Long Salts would become ill, begin to waste away, then die in suffering. To the wiser, more astute individuals of the family (which at that time numbered more than a hundred members) it was becoming increasingly obvious that someone had set a Chindi upon them. But why?

At last the two lazy ones confessed substituting the wild antelope for the mutton. After a council of family leaders, it was agreed that certain of their members would meet with the medicine priest and confront the situation without further delay.

The blind medicine man admitted that he had become very angry when he discovered the deception that had been worked upon him by the Long Salts. He also admitted that he had set a Chindi against them with the instructions that the entire family should be exterminated one by one.

The representatives of the Long Salts beseeched the medicine man to grant them a reprieve and to recall the avenging spirit: "You must understand that we also were duped by those lazy and deceitful members of our family. We did not mean to cheat you. We fully intended to keep our bargain with you."

The blind medicine priest listened carefully to their words, evaluating their sincerity.

"Already several of our family have died," one of the elder Long Salts pointed out. "Surely you would now consider yourself avenged for such a simple matter as five sheep. We will give you ten sheep, twenty sheep, thirty sheep. Name your price and call off the Chindi!"

The old medicine priest raised his hand for silence. He had been touched by their pleas and by their argument that the deception had not been a deliberate one on the part of the entire Long Salt family.

"I am not an evil man," he told them, "but you must see that I was forced to uphold my dignity and my reputation."

The Long Salt family representatives quickly consented that they understood the principle involved in his exacting revenge.

"I will remove the curse," the blind medicine priest nodded slowly. "But I must charge you a price. You understand that I am required to do so according to the same law that required me to set the Chindi upon you."

An elder Long Salt said that they would not question his judgment. "We understand that all things must have a price if they are to be of consequence. Name your price. We will pay what you ask."

The old priest motioned for his son to come to his side. "I am very tired now," he told the assembled Long Salts. "At the moment, I cannot think of what the proper price should be to call off the Chindi. Please return in ten days. We will agree to the terms at that time."

The Long Salts were dismayed at being put off for such a period. How many more of their family would die in the meantime? On the other hand, they knew better than to protest the old priest's decision, for he might become impatient and allow the Chindi full rein to kill all the Long Salts one by one.

On the morning of the tenth day, the delegation from the Long Salts was prompt in keeping its appointment. In respectful silence it arrived at the hogan of the blind medicine man.

The Long Salts were greeted by a family in mourning. The old medicine priest had passed to the land of the spirits three days earlier.

"But please tell us," they begged the priest's son, "did he recall the Chindi that he had set upon us? Did he call off the spirit before he died?"

To the Long Salts' horror, they were unable to determine whether or not the medicine priest had summoned the Chindi back to its lair of darkness before his unexpected death.

"I know that he had thought much about the problem," the son told them. "But I do not know if he was able to call back the Chindi before he went to the land of the grandfathers."

By the time the Long Salts had returned home they had their answer. Several members of the family lay ill and dying.

✛

In the August–September 1967 issue of *Frontier Times*, John R. Winslowe wrote that he met the last surviving member of the Long Salts in 1925, a slender teenaged girl named Alice: "Curiously, anyone marrying into the family met the same fate as a blood Long Salt. Alice's mother died when the girl reached seven and she was attending the Tuba City boarding school at the Indian agency. Alice's father became skin and bones, dying two years later.... The remaining three Long Salts [Alice's two uncles and an aunt] were ill, crippled, and helpless. Friends cared for them, watching them fade into nothing before their eyes."

Alice had been the top student in her class at the agency school, but within a few months of the death of the last of her relatives, her teachers noted Alice becoming dull and listless. Soon she was ill with a malady that defied the medical doctor's conventional methods of diagnosis.

An aging but determined Navajo man named Hosteen Behegade adopted Alice Long Salt and resolved that he would protect her from the Chindi's efforts to destroy the sole surviving member of a once proud family. Behegade was incensed that so many people had had to die because of the deceit of two lazy men who tried to

trick a blind old medicine man. His sense of justice was outraged that such awful vengeance had been exacted for the sake of five butchered sheep. The stubborn Navajo declared his defiance to the Chindi.

Although Behegade was considered rather well-off with a respectable number of sheep, horses, and cattle, Navajo medicine priests conducted sings for him free of charge.

Rallying to his example of bravery, each of the medicine men earnestly desired to be the one whose abilities could at last thwart the Chindi.

By late 1927, however, the defiant Behegade was still fighting courageously for Alice's life, but he had lost all of his property and was heavily in debt.

Behegade had, however, evolved a plan. According to John Winslowe, Behegade reasoned that in order to finish off the stricken girl, the Chindi had to be present. "His idea was to keep moving constantly, concealing his trail. By this means, he could prevent the Chindi from locating Alice.

"One night an owl hooted close by. At dawn Alice Long Salt was too weak to leave her blankets. The Chindi had found its innocent victim again. From then on, Behegade always obeyed the owl's hoot, believing that it had come to his aid against the Chindi."

In the winter of 1928, the fearful wanderers found themselves seeking refuge from a blizzard in a hogan three miles from the trading post on Red Mesa. Alice seemed to rally in health and she became cheerful. Perhaps the blizzard would protect them. Surely the Chindi could not find them amid the deep-piling snow and the howling wind.

The blizzard developed into the worst snowstorm in years. The Behegade family relaxed its guard and slept peacefully. Not even a Chindi could combat such a violent working of the elements.

The next morning, Alice Long Salt was dead. The final propitiation had been exacted. At last the Chindi would return to whatever realm it had come from, its one-hundred-year mission of vengeance completed.

# CHAPTER THREE

# THE CURSE OF THE OWL PROPHET

Maman-ti, He-Who-Touches-the-Sky, earned the name Owl Prophet because it was the owl that became his totem, his familiar spirit, and it was the owl that would come to tell him the outcome of future battles. Owl Prophet was esteemed by his people, the Kiowa, and was so highly regarded by their allies that the Comanches named him to the position of master of all medicine men.

Owl Prophet, Maman-ti, has been described as a tall, aristocratic man, a warrior-priest who was revered not only for the power of his medicine but as a man of courage who fought in the most important battles. In addition, he had a reputation as a daring guerrilla strategist.

While the council chiefs sat in silence, Maman-ti would listen to the screeching cries of an owl sounding from somewhere in the darkness. There would be the beating of wings, an interlude of silence while Owl Prophet sat in meditation, then he would interpret the message he had received from his totem spirit.

Brad first heard the story of the Owl Prophet when he was traveling among various tribes in the early 1970s, collecting accounts of medicine priests who had accomplished great acts of magic. Among many of the old ones, some of whom claimed to have been very small children when the last of the *bronco* (renegade) holdouts were corralled by the U.S. cavalry, still regarded Maman-ti, the

Owl Prophet, as a hero. We must remember that those last few war-riors who refused to be sent to the reservations were regarded as freedom fighters by their people.

By the late 1860s, the Kiowa and their allies had been battered, scattered, and defeated by the pony soldiers, the yellowlegs, with their inexhaustible supplies of men, weapons, and ammunition. Many of the great war leaders had been killed, and the death song had been sung far too many times in the camps of the tribes who stubbornly resisted the encroachment of the white men. It seemed as though the greedy invaders could never be contented at sunset with what they had had at sunrise.

In 1870, the mighty chief Kicking Bird had assessed the situation of the Kiowa as becoming increasingly futile, and he urged large numbers of his people and their allied tribes to save their lives and to join him in the settlement outside Fort Sill, Oklahoma. Although there seemed wisdom in what Kicking Bird said for the old, the very young, and the ill, Long Wolf, Owl Prophet, White Horse, and a few other chiefs continued to lead small bands of warriors on raids into Texas and to wage guerrilla warfare against the numeri-cally superior bluecoats.

Life as "outlaw Indians," always on the run, always pursued by a relentless enemy who regarded them as savage animals, provid-ed an existence of unimaginable hardships and terrors. The rene-gade bands managed to harass the bluecoats and elude the angry columns of vengeful troopers again and again.

Finally, however, by February 1875, Kicking Bird managed to convince even these determined resistance leaders to break their arrows and to set aside their rifles.

Although Kicking Bird was regarded as a great peacemaker by his white benefactors, his own tribe, who had vowed to continue to fight to the last warrior, saw him as a creature worthy only of their contempt. For five years, Kicking Bird and his family had lived in a comfortable lodge near a bluecoat fort while his friends and their allies maintained a war that had been his responsibility to support.

"Many of our people feel that Kicking Bird should be killed," Long Wolf said to Owl Prophet. "They say that you should be

chief. Your medicine has never failed, and your courageous loyalty to the tribe is without question."

Owl Prophet thanked his friend for the words of praise but advised against the murder of Kicking Bird. "Although I do not agree with our brother, I see that he feels that he has our people's best interests at heart. He has seen his visions and obeyed his medicine as he understands them. We must work in union with him for the good of the people."

Owl Prophet would probably have been instrumental in healing the breach between the two factions of the Kiowa if the fiery and vengeful bluecoat leader General Sherman had not decreed that certain of the recently surrendered Indians must be punished for their recalcitrance. The officers at Fort Sill, perhaps more sensitive to the situation than the warring Sherman, found themselves in a quandary as they attempted to decide which of their prisoners should be most eligible for long-term imprisonment. Regretfully, they turned the disagreeable task over to Kicking Bird and told him to select twenty-six Kiowa for banishment to the dungeons of Fort Marion, Florida.

With a sad heart and with great concern for the future harmony of the tribe, Kicking Bird complied with the orders of the military authorities. Because of the notorious record of their repeated raids into Texas he chose Long Wolf, Owl Prophet, Woman's Heart, and White Horse—then rounded out the remainder of the quota with a random selection of warriors and a few Mexican captives who had been reared with the allied tribes. Although those closest to Kicking Bird knew that he had obeyed the white man's decree with a heavy heart, many of the chiefs and warriors who had once been among his most loyal followers now came to regard him as a traitor and a heartless opportunist.

On April 28, 1875, as the chained prisoners were being loaded into wagons for the long trip to Florida, Kicking Bird rode up and told the men how much he regretted his part in their exile.

"You must believe how sorry I am," Kicking Bird said, his normally rich, steady baritone quavering into a plea for understanding. "I love you, and I will work for your release."

Long Wolf seemed little impressed with Kicking Bird's sentiments and his promise to work for their parole. He held up his chained wrists and swung the metal links together in a discordant beat of protest. "Chains do not mean love to me," he said.

"I am sorry," Kicking Bird replied, now on the defensive. "I am sorry that you are in chains, Long Wolf. But it is because of your stubbornness that you did not keep out of trouble. It is because you continued to lead raids into Texas. Now you will have to be punished by the government."

Maman-ti, the Owl Prophet, had not lost his ability as an orator, and he delivered a scornful diatribe toward the chief he considered a traitor.

"The laws of the bluecoats are not our laws," he reminded Kicking Bird. "We are ruled by the Great Mystery, not the Great White Father who sends pony soldiers after us because we wish only to be Kiowa. You may think that you are now a big man among the white people. You may think that you are special to the Great Mystery because you live free while we are bound in chains. You may find glory in your comfortable lodge while we are sent to a land from which few of us are likely to return. But Kicking Bird, hear this: I loved you above all men. I served you faithfully. I returned to Fort Sill because you asked it of me. I spoke against those who would have had you killed for your betrayal of our people.

"Now I say this: Cherish every sunset, every sunrise, every caress of your woman and every touch of your children, for I shall return and kill you with my own hands."

Two days later on the miserable journey, Eagle Chief, a medicine man of high ability, managed to find a seat near Owl Prophet.

"I heard you promise to kill Kicking Bird with your hands," Eagle Chief said. "That was a threat made only of the wind of your breath. You will not be able to kill Kicking Bird."

Anger flared within Owl Prophet "I do not make weak threats of my breath. I shall kill Kicking Bird with my hands, as I have said it."

Eagle Chief laughed. "You are too wise to say such foolish things. You are the greatest of all medicine men. Surely your vision has shown you that none of us will survive in this faraway prison of the white man."

Owl Prophet shifted uneasily on the hard wooden seat. He had not permitted himself a glimpse of the future. He had not wished to foresee the shadows of death that might await them in a place so foreign to the Kiowa.

Eagle Chief leaned closer and spoke with great fervor. "You do not need to wait to kill Kicking Bird with your hands. You have the medicine to kill him from a great distance."

Owl Prophet looked deep into the eyes of his medicine brother. "The death prayer?"

Eagle Chief nodded solemnly.

Owl Prophet sat for several moments in silence. "You know," he spoke at last, "that my medicine forbids me to use the death prayer against a fellow Kiowa. If I should ever sing the death prayer for one of my own people, my medicine has revealed that I too shall die."

"How much life will there be for you in a Florida prison?" Eagle Chief replied.

Owl Prophet said no more. Eagle Chief interpreted his silence as withdrawal, and he turned away from his tribesman, fearful that he had said too much.

That night as they camped and the wagons had been quiet for many hours, the Kiowa heard the keening wail of the death prayer. None of them needed to speak; they all knew that Owl Prophet was making good his vow of death to Kicking Bird.

Two mornings later, back at Fort Sill, Kicking Bird collapsed in great pain after drinking a cup of coffee. He died just before noon, while the agency doctor stood helplessly at his bedside. The physician had checked the cup for signs of poison and found none. He had no explanation why a healthy, robust, forty-year-old man should suddenly drop dead.

Owl Prophet uttered a sigh of resignation when word of Kicking Bird's death eventually reached the wagonloads of prisoners.

"It is accomplished," Long Wolf said aloud, and the other Kiowa began to sing their own personal songs in recognition of the retribution they had all witnessed.

Owl Prophet leaned back against the jarring side of the buckboard. He would now endure the discomforts of travel willingly. The dungeons of Fort Marion no longer held any threat for him. Owl Prophet knew that he would never live to see the iron bars of any prison cell.

According to the official report of the U.S. Army, Owl Prophet died of natural causes before the journey to Florida had ended.

CHAPTER FOUR

# THE GHOSTLY MISSION OF SAN ANTONIO DE PADUA

Monks at one of America's oldest missions are convinced that their religious center is enchanted. They and archaeologists working at the site have seen and heard ghosts, have experienced spiritual events that have changed people's lives, and have seen mysterious colored clouds hovering just above the mission on baking-hot, cloudless days.

"This is a highly spiritual place," observed Franciscan brother Timothy Arthur, historian at California's lonely Mission of San Antonio de Padua. "There is no evil here, but a lot of spiritual happenings. Even when the first padres came here in 1770 there were mysteries about the area. Local Indians told them of monks just like them who had come before—flying through the air."

The mission, constructed in 1771, is located in the central California mountains of the Santa Lucia range, thirty miles north of Paso Robles. A nearby U.S. Army base is the only other settlement. Each year several dozen people go to the remote mission for spiritual refreshment, staying a week or more.

On one occasion in the mid-1980s, Brother Timothy recalled having been in the refectory with some archaeologists when they all heard someone moving in the attic above them.

"We could hear the footsteps taking a few paces, then stepping over the crossbeams, and we thought that it was an intruder," he

recalled. "Two of the young archaeologists went up, one to the door at each end, and searched with flashlights. Nobody was there, and the thick dust was totally undisturbed. We don't know *what* it was, but it wasn't human."

Richard Senate, a city archaeologist for Ventura, California, told journalist Paul Bannister of his other worldly experience while working at the mission:

"I had been classifying material and I was walking through the courtyard to get a cold drink from the icebox. It was about twelve-thirty A.M.

"I saw, through the dense blackness, a light on the other side of the courtyard and I realized that it was a candle. I changed my course to see who it was, because the monks are strict about restricting use of candles because of the fire hazard. I was about twelve feet from the figure, and I opened my mouth to speak.

"The person was wearing a monk's habit and was less than average height. We were both approaching the door to the chapel—then he vanished!

"I flicked on my flashlight, but there was nothing there. He couldn't have quietly opened the door, because it is heavy and it squeaks. There was only blank wall around.

"I didn't believe in ghosts until then. Now I do.

"I found out later that the timing of the ghost's appearance had been significant. The old padres would get up about twelve-thirty A.M. and pray in the chapel for an hour and go back to bed. I'm convinced that I saw a three-dimensional image from the past—a psychic echo of a dead monk going to prayer."

The monks of Mission San Antonio de Padua have several times seen a small colored cloud, about three feet square and about eight feet high above the tile roof over the women's guest quarters.

"I have seen it myself, changing colors, as if someone were behind it with colored lights." Brother Timothy said. "There have been no other clouds in the sky, just that little one going from white to green to blue, then yellow and red. I have never been

able to find an explanation for it."

The monks tell of the day Father John Baptist died and a similar mysterious cloud appeared that seemed to signal the clergyman's passing.

Father John had been working in Atascadero, seventy miles away from the mission, when he died, and the monks had not yet gotten the news. Brother Timothy remembered that a wispy white cloud floated out of the door of the winter chapel.

Father Joe saw it as well, and the two of them watched its eerie movements.

"The cloud went along the cloister, then turned abruptly along the path," Brother Timothy said. "As we watched it, it went out to the fountain at the center of the courtyard, hovered there for a minute or two, then turned again and went along another path, along a cloister, and into the church. I ran to follow it, but it had disappeared inside."

The two clerics noted that the white cloud had followed the exact route Father John had followed each day on his way to say his noon office. He had always walked the same path, even pausing to feed the goldfish in the fountain. Brother Timothy and Father Joe are convinced that Father John's soul was following his familiar path one more time.

On numerous occasions in recent years the mission has been the scene of remarkable spiritual conversions. In one instance, a young man named Aldo, who had been involved in drug-dealing, had come to attempt to clear his conscience.

He was staying in the room that had been recently inhabited by Katherine, an English woman with terminal cancer who had returned to her home in England to die. Katherine had spent time at the mission in order to prepare her soul for her transition.

At the exact time that Katherine died in England, Aldo told how he was awakened by a dazzlingly bright light. "I was paralyzed, fixed to my bed for several minutes," he told the monks later. Then the light dimmed, and he was able to move.

Brother Timothy remembered how the monks had returned with the young man to his room. "We could see the outline of his body in his own perspiration. Later we found out about Katherine's death. We also learned that Aldo is now leading an exemplary life."

In a similar case, the parents of another young man, Richard, were staying at the mission. In dismay and disgust, they had left him to go his own way, and he was in trouble with the police. Richard was in one room, his parents in the next, when the building began to tremble and shake. At first none of them could move, then they ran into the courtyard to escape the earthquake.

But they soon discovered that nobody else had felt any tremors—even though the quake had been so powerful in their rooms that furniture had been overturned.

Richard's parents took the violent manifestation as a sign that they should no longer ignore their son's needs, and the monks testified that they are now a close and loving family unit. Richard is out of trouble and plans to stay that way.

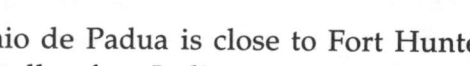

The Mission of San Antonio de Padua is close to Fort Hunter Liggett, and a local legend tells of an Indian woman who was decapitated by her husband near what is now the army base. Over the years there have been numerous reports from soldiers on guard duty of seeing a headless woman on horseback.

Brother Timothy remembered one dramatic report from a few years back: "Four military police in two jeeps saw such a figure near the base's ammunition supply point. They chased her, but she disappeared. They described her as wearing a long cloak, and they said she simply disappeared into thin air near the Gavilan Impact Area."

The monks of San Antonio de Padua have their own favorite supernatural tale, about Gigi Giardino, a seven-year-old, whom they call their "own little angel."

When Gigi's mother was told that her daughter was dying of cancer and that she only had fourteen days to live before she would go into a coma and die, she brought the child to the mission so that she might have a peaceful end to her life. It was also the little girl's wish that she might be buried there.

But the monks could not receive permission from clerical authorities to permit such a burial on mission grounds. "We tried and we tried to get a dispensation to bury her, but proceedings dragged on," Brother Timothy said. "Yet Gigi did not die. For twenty-nine long days she remained in her coma. Then permission arrived. The very next day, the child died.

"We buried her in a quiet corner of the courtyard garden, and soon after her grave was covered with wild purple violets—a flower that will *not* grow here because it is too hot."

Brother Timothy tended the miracle violets for nine years. "They bloomed regularly. Then, about a year ago, I found them all dead."

Father Joe and Brother Timothy discussed the strange death of the purple violets and talked about placing more flowers on Gigi's grave.

"But we need not have worried," Brother Timothy continued. "A week later, a mass of white violets had mysteriously appeared on Gigi's grave. Within a few days we had a letter telling us that Gigi's mother had died. We know that the sudden appearance of the white violets was a sign, because now both purple and white violets grow intermingled on that small grave. These are signs from Heaven, I am certain. They are an affirmation of our faith."

Professor Robert Hoover, professor of archaeology at California Polytechnic/San Luis Obispo, who has conducted many digs at the mission over a period of eight years, described the Mission of San Antonio de Padua as constituting one of the longest-inhabited buildings in the United States.

"It is a very spiritual place," Professor Hoover told journalist Paul Bannister. "It has an aura of the paranormal about it. I think there is truth in the ghost stories. The headless horsewoman, for

example, has a documented history. I also know of people on digs at the mission who have reported mysterious happenings. Brother Timothy has done considerable research into the legends that surround the mission, and I'd say that it is certainly a very haunted place."

According to Professor Hoover, one student, who was studying at the University of California/Santa Cruz, reported being unable to move when a bright light came into his room. "He didn't know what to think. It was just one of many incidents at the old mission."

# CHAPTER FIVE

# MYSTERY WINDS AND EXPLOSIONS FROM NOWHERE

The Arizona rancher sat upright in his bed, clutched his startled wife, then swung both feet onto the chilly winter floor.

"My God, Cal!" his wife gasped. "What was *that*?"

"The old barrel we keep the tractor gasoline in must have exploded," he answered as he shrugged into a flannel shirt and snagged his jeans off a bedside chair. "I'm gonna run out and get the stock out of the barn. It's sure to be on fire. Dorothy, you call the fire department in town and tell them to blow that siren good and loud and to get out here fast!"

"It sure is funny that we can't see any flames," Dorothy said, reaching for her robe.

The rancher noted his wife's observation and scowled. He walked to the window and looked out.

It was a clear night with a full moon and bright stars. He could plainly see the gas barrel sitting perfectly intact atop its makeshift tower. The livestock were beginning to settle down, but their German shepherd pup was still howling its complaint at whatever had shattered the stillness of a crisp winter night.

"So what in hell was it?," The rancher intoned softly. "There's no smoke, no fire. Do you suppose it was one of them damn sonic booms from some big jet at Luke Air Force Base?"

✜

"Big jets" that are never spotted, earthquakes that are never recorded on seismographs, explosives that never leave debris, and UFOs emerging from other dimensions are the suspects most often named by those who have suffered property damage and who have had the blazes scared out of them by mystery blasts and explosions from nowhere that have been reported throughout the United States, but with unusual frequency in certain areas of the Southwest.

In Modesto, California, on October 3, 1950, a mystery explosion shattered the night with such violence that a general fire alarm was sounded for fifteen miles around.

✜

In May 1951, the Rock Solaneo and Contra districts of San Francisco were shaken with undetermined explosions for a period of two weeks. The ground shook, windows rattled and cracked, and pictures fell as the entire area was rocked by blasts, explosions, shocks, and jars.

The San Francisco *Examiner* stated that its reporters had checked "military facilities in the area, quarries, contractors, city and county officials, every commercial operation which uses explosions" and found them all as mystified as anyone else.

According to the *Examiner*, the mystery blasts usually began around 9:00 A.M. and sometimes as many as a dozen would shake the area in a single day. The mysterious explosions were heard in all parts of Vallejo and across Carquinex Strait in Contra Costa County.

On June fifteenth, a blast of undetermined origin separated the causeway connecting Mare Island to the mainland. This mystery blast took place at 3:00 P.M. and rattled several buildings. Day-shift workers at Mare Island were delayed on their way home while a crack several inches wide was filled.

Investigating naval and shipyard personnel considered clue after clue to the explosion, and thoroughly explored both the suggestion

of sabotage and the accusation that an air force practice bomb might have gone astray. Sabotage was eliminated, and air force officers at the Fourth Air Force and at Hamilton Field countered the veiled accusation directed at them with a strong denial.

As far as the public has ever been informed, investigators were unable to discover a single acceptable explanation for the mystery blast at Mare Island.

On January 4, 1952, a series of unknown blasts shook Los Angeles and San Diego. The first explosion sounded at 3:33 A.M. in the vicinity of Los Angeles International Airport. The second thundered forth from San Diego's Mission Hills at 8:30 P.M., followed by a third at Point Loma half an hour later, and a fourth nearly two hours later in the Chula Vista region, thus encompassing an area of about thirty miles. Witnesses described the mystery blasts as sounding like deep, rolling thunder—or the "steady barrage of far-away cannon." Police officials stated that their investigation revealed that no explosions had been set off at those times. Scientists selected the convenient old scapegoat of exploding meteorites, even though none had been reported or observed on that date.

In the summer of 1959, a violent shock accompanied by two loud explosions was reported in an area from one hundred miles northeast of Amarillo, Texas, to Roswell, New Mexico, two hundred miles to the southeast. In Pampa, a town fifty-five miles northeast of Amarillo, the wall of a downtown building was cracked by the blasts.

Seismograph stations said the shock could not have been caused by an earth tremor. Further inquiry determined that no supersonic flights had been scheduled over the area at the time of the mysterious explosions. If the mystery blasts are not caused by earthquakes or by sonic booms in the sky, just where can their point of origin be?

31

Unexplained blasts in the sky over the San Francisco area in a three-day period that same summer knocked dishes from shelves and cracked the plaster on innumerable household walls. Windows were shattered over a thirty-five-mile area; and the unidentified explosions were also held responsible for opening the door to a bank vault, triggering fire alarms, and setting off a warehouse sprinkler system.

On the night of August 18, 1962, many San Franciscans thought that an airborne armada of enemy bombers was clouding the skies above their city. Between 10:00 and 10:30 P.M., a mysterious rumbling noise that sounded like the flight of heavy superbombers came from somewhere above San Francisco.

Navy spokesmen from Alameda Naval Air Station denied running any engines after 10:00 P.M.

A theory that atmospheric conditions could have been "just right" to magnify thunderclaps fell through when authorities were reminded that the evening of August 18 was clear, with virtually no wind.

Nor was there any wind on U.S. Route 75 between Madisonville and Centerville, Texas, on April 19, 1963, when Louis A. Johnson of Houston was returning from a trip to Fort Worth; but that did not prevent *something* from lifting his automobile into the air, turning it completely around, and setting it back down on the highway traveling the opposite direction from which he had come.

Johnson, a World War II Marine Corps veteran, said that his unexpected and unexplainable ride was more exciting than anything he had experienced in two invasions.

"I can't even describe the sensation," he said. "When I realized what had happened, and that I'd come down partly on the shoulder of the road, I put the car into lower gear and eased to a stop. I didn't think the car had been hurt any, but when I got to Houston I stopped at a service station and they found that the oil pump wasn't working too well."

Several eyewitnesses saw Johnson's automobile suddenly take

flight, become airborne, and in an attempt to fit what they had seen into some understandable form of reality, most of them believed that a tornado had swooped down and momentarily hoisted him aloft.

There was no tornado, of course, and there are few dust devils or sudden whirlwinds that could elevate a two-ton automobile into the air. And probably no tornado would set an automobile back down on the highway without considerable damage to either car or occupant.

Yet something did lift Johnson's automobile into the air. Could it have been the same *something* responsible for the mystery blasts? Is it possible that some force not visible to the human eye is soaring around breaking the sound barrier with horrendous sonic booms—and occasionally reaching down to pluck up an automobile?

❖

About the same time in the spring of 1963 that Louis Johnson's automobile became airborne on a Texas highway, an invisible force ripped off the roof of an apartment building on Shenandoah Street in Hollywood, California, and scattered it in pieces up to 280 feet away. In the floors below, Mrs. Bertha Fink was left lying in bed trying to figure out why a spring rain was falling directly on her; Mrs. Rachael Benveniste was tossed out of her bed; and Mrs. Sarah Eisenberg was startled to find her ceiling suddenly cracked and leaking water.

Authorities did their best to classify the mystery force as a sonic boom, a gas explosion, or a small tornado—depending upon which expert was quoted. Extensive investigation by gas-company officials determined that their utility was not the culprit. The weather bureau denied the existence of a tornado that might have struck Hollywood on that particular evening. And everyone wondered if a sonic boom could really be capable of ripping away a roof from an apartment building.

But we all know that strange things do happen in Hollywood, and mysterious sonic booms and weird, unexplainable objects that fall from the sky may simply be a part of the bizarre repertoire of one of the world's most high-energy cities.

33

On April 25, 1968, a Lakewood, California, man, Bert Martin, watched a large hunk of ice falling out of a clear sky above a Hollywood streetcorner. There were no tall buildings near the corner and no airplanes visible overhead. The largest fragment of ice weighed twenty-five pounds.

Those who make a serious study of such phenomena are quick to point out that such mysterious ghostly blasts, strange and powerful winds, and inexplicable skyfalls date back to the earliest records of exploring the Southwest and even to Indian legends of the area. Unfortunately, an uninformed public and an entrenched science regard a great deal of such documentation as pure, unadulterated kookery. But neither, it seems, do the skeptics offer explanations acceptable to the individuals who have endured mystery blasts and such phenomena as glowing, and sometimes fatal, rain.

In 1961, a rainfall near Huixtla in Chiapas state, Mexico, that killed several children, according to United Press International. When the deadly liquid touched human skin, it produced blisters that later became dark stains resembling hot oil burns.

On the Wednesday before Christmas 1965 it rained in Buckeye, Arizona. According to the old-timers and the weather bureau, rain during the holiday season is unusual enough, but this rain left glowing spots on the ground that varied from a quarter of an inch to two inches in diameter.

Buckeye Civil Defense Director George Hamner checked the spots with a Geiger counter and was relieved to find that it registered no harmful radioactivity.

Jerry Benson, a high school biology teacher, told reporters that he had at first suspected the glowing rain spots to be composed of aluminum. "But on taking a real close look at them, they appeared

to have a pale-green glow. The first time that I walked across my backyard, I didn't see anything, but the more that I looked, the more spots I saw.

"I don't believe that the rain activated spots of phosphorus in the soil," Benson went on. "An earthworm that got covered with the stuff turned into a glowworm!"

On April 16, 1968, seventeen-year-old Louis Duenweg and three friends discovered strange whitish blobs bobbing at the water's edge along Huntington Beach, California. Duenweg broke one of the things open to examine better the unfamiliar pinkish substance within the plasticlike shell. There was a sudden hissing noise; and before the teenager could drop the thing and run, the blob exploded, temporarily blinding him and burning his face.

About a week later, another young man scooped a similar object out of the sea along Seal Beach. He cracked it open, became disinterested in his find, tossed it over his shoulder. The resultant blast knocked him to the beach and made a small crater in the sand.

Quite naturally, swimmers, sunbathers, surfers, fishermen, and coastal residents become a bit uptight when mysterious, unidentified explosive globs are found floating off their beaches.

Military spokesmen insisted that they were not in any way responsible for the blasting blobs from the ocean.

The Los Angeles County crime laboratory was said to have fished a number of blobs out of the ocean for careful analysis, but apparently no official report was ever released that identified the explosive globule's place of origin.

But then who could identify the place of origin of the monkey that fell from the sky over California?

On October 26, 1956, Mrs. Faye Swanson of Broadmoor, California, stepped out into her backyard at 8:05 A.M. and discovered the body of a small, furry monkey that had fallen out of the sky during the night and crashed into her clothesline with such force that a solid four-by-four post had splintered. Investigators on the scene determined that the angle at which the body of the pri-

mate had struck the wooden post indicated that it could only have fallen from above

A spokesperson from San Francisco International Airport said that no airliner had been transporting monkeys during the night. No authority from any other organization could offer an explanation for the origin of the monkey that had dropped in from the clouds. The San Francisco *Chronicle* headlined the question: "WHO'S THROWING MONKEYS AT THE EARTH?"

As wise pundits have long agreed what goes up, must come down. However, it seems as though some invisible, incredible force has up and down, in and out, backward and forward slightly mixed up.

# CHAPTER SIX

# WELCOME TO TWILIGHT ZONE, TEXAS

The two teenagers embraced in the lovers' lane. They had just come from a summer movie in White Rock Lake, a small town just outside Dallas. Though the young man's attention was riveted on the pretty girl in his arms, he could not help catching a glimmer of white moving down the narrow road toward them.

"Maybe it's the nosy cops spoiling everyone's fun," he growled impatiently.

The couple watched as the shimmering white light grew in size and intensity.

"Jeez," the boy whispered between his teeth. "Look at that!"

The shimmering white light had become a figure—the figure of a woman. The girl at his side screamed as the ghostly woman walked directly toward their car. She appeared to be wearing an evening gown and she was dripping wet from head to toe.

The teenagers watched in horror as the figure stood at the side of the car and reached for the door handle on the passenger side. The young driver turned the ignition key with shaking fingers and floored the accelerator, sending dirt and stones flying into the branches behind the car. When he glanced in the mirror, he could no longer see the ghostly white lady.

✢

The Lady of the Lake has frequently been seen wandering in the area of White Rock Lake, Texas. Numerous newspaper articles have been written about this eerie wraith over the years, and the consensus seems to be that the ghost represents a woman who was drowned accidently—or on purpose—in the lake.

Most of the accounts of the apparition come from lovers' lane couples or late-night drivers, who see her appear along the side of the road. According to some who have encountered her "face-to-face," she appears to be jealous of the young lovers and wishes to frighten them out of their amorous activities. If that is her purpose, she is usually quite successful. One young man said that he would never forget the sight of the shimmering ghost staring in the car window at him and his frightened date.

Drivers who have stopped to investigate, supposing that they have come upon a woman in trouble, say that she leaves only a puddle of water where she had stood at the side of the road.

Dale Berry told Frank X. Tolbert, columnist for the Dallas *Morning News*, that they received a house call from the Lady of the Lake when they purchased a house near White Rock Lake in September 1962. On their first night in their new home, Berry hurried to the door to answer the ringing of the bell. There was no one there. The bell rang a second time. In spite of a rapid dash to the door, whoever had rung the bell had vanished.

The third time the bell rang, Berry's daughter answered the door. Soon the entire family was clustered around the front door in response to the girl's screams. On the porch were large puddles of water, as if someone dripping wet had stood there. There were large droplets of water on the steps and on the walk leading up to the front door. The sprinkler system had not been turned on, and the rest of the yard was dry. The night was clear and cloudless. Moreover, the neighbors were not the sort to indulge in practical jokes.

It appeared that the White Lady of White Rock Lake had been trying to pay the newcomers a welcoming visit.

The Lone Star state is filled with such tales of visitors from their own brand of twilight zone and of accounts of people and things that appear and disappear.

Thomas Phillips of Pasadena, Texas, told of the time on January 10, 1960, when on a business trip, he stopped for a train between Belleville and Sealy. He first saw the train coming off to his right, about three hundred feet ahead. Strangely enough, the train, pulled by an old-style locomotive, had seemed to move out of a cloud of fog.

As he drummed his fingers impatiently on the steering wheel waiting for the train to pass, Phillips suddenly realized that there were no crossing lights, signs, or signals. As the freight cars passed slowly in front of him, he also noticed that the train seemed to be lighted "by a source entirely apart from the lights of [his] car."

When the last boxcar passed before him, to his surprise Phillips saw that "there was no sign of railroad bed, not even a break in the pavement where one had ever been."

✛

In July 1984 Mr. and Mrs. Harold Davidson were on a vacation trip in the Corpus Christi area when they spotted an attractive house on the outskirts of the city, which they hoped might be for rent.

"It appeared to be quite vacant, and it would have so nicely suited our purposes," Davidson said. "We both like to dabble in oils as amateur painters, and the house would have afforded us a nice view of the ocean.

"It was two-story, rather substantial-looking," he went on. "We judged the style of architecture to date from the late 1870s or early 1880s. It had a fresh, trim appearance, but we especially loved the groves of lilac bushes and the beautiful flower gardens that were so well-tended.

"We were in a bit of rush that afternoon, so we made careful note of the place and decided to come back that evening and make inquiries regarding its rental for the summer."

When the Davidsons returned late that afternoon, they found

nothing but empty sandy fields running down toward the ocean.

"We had taken careful note of the locality of the house," Davidson said. "We drove all over the area, but we saw nothing even resembling that magnificent old house. When we spoke to the nearest neighbors, we could find no one who had even a memory of such a house ever having been in the neighborhood."

In June 1986, Lyle Mortensen was returning with his family from a picnic with some friends outside Galveston when he became annoyed with the way in which the old Model-T Ford in front of them was slowing traffic.

"I figured it was someone going or coming to some antique auto show," he said, "but I thought it peculiar that he didn't have those special license plates that you're supposed to have on those old cars. I wanted to be tolerant and all, but I did have to get back home because I had to go to work early the next morning. I hated to do it, but I really hit down on my horn and gave him a terrible blast to get out of my way."

Mortensen recalled that the driver of the Model-T seemed to jump as if truly startled or frightened by the sound of his horn. The man turned to look at them, and Mortensen saw that his eyes were wide with seeming terror.

"Then the car just seemed to drift sideways off the road, like it was floating, and it went off into the ditch," Mortensen said. "'My God, what have I done?' I cried out to my wife. 'I've made the guy leave the road. I've got to go back and see if he's all right.'"

But as the Mortensens swung back and pulled alongside the Model T, the old automobile disappeared in front of their eyes. "It just faded away like an old photograph dissolving bit by bit until there wasn't anything left to prove that it had ever been there. It had completely vanished in about thirty seconds."

On May 15, 1987, Sam and Clara Carter were traveling to Amarillo during the early morning hours. A few miles east of the

city they stopped to eat at a quaint rustic-style restaurant neither of them had ever noticed on any of their previous trips to the region.

The food was excellent down-home cooking, and the waitress and the cook were so friendly in a charming, folksy manner that the Carters truly meant their promise to stop back again. In fact, they tried to do just that on their return drive, but the restaurant was nowhere to be seen.

The Carters traveled that route three successive weekends searching for the friendly little restaurant with the wonderful down-home cooking, but it had simply vanished into nothingness.

"Since then, we have journeyed that highway many times," Sam Carter reported, "but we never again have found that terrific little restaurant."

Many students of the paranormal are familiar with the strange case of the television call letters KLEE-TV of Houston, Texas, which appeared on the home screen of Mr. H. C. Taylor, a specialist in long-distance television reception in Lancashire, England. Now the very fact that Taylor somehow managed to pull in a signal from such a faraway spot as Houston is extremely noteworthy, but it is not the point of the story.

Taylor received the signal in September 1953. The KLEE call letters had not been broadcast since July 1950, when the Houston station changed its call letters to KPRC.

Quite understandably, the chief engineer of KPRC doubted Taylor's claim, but he later admitted that the photograph Taylor sent him did indeed show the old KLEE call letters on the standard call-letter slide utilized by the station.

Nearly everyone in this electronic age is aware of the fact that television emissions can occasionally be picked up at enormous distances from their point of transmission due to unusual atmospheric conditions. Perhaps no one can adequately explain precisely why such things may happen from time to time, but they occur often enough to allow us to accept them simply as unusual but not startling.

In this case, we must repeat that the perplexing reception occurred in 1953—long before communications satellites and mammoth receiving disks were a part of media technology. Also, it would seem that the very notion that a station's call letters could be picked up three years after their final broadcast would have to fit into the "startling" category.

Some very sane and sober theorists did suggest the possibility that the broadcast waves from KLEE might somehow have penetrated the ionosphere and not rebounded until they finally hit a celestial object several light years away.

In any case, on November 25, 1955, two years later, Taylor tuned in his set for long-range reception and once again saw before him the call letters KLEE-TV—broadcasting, no doubt, from Twilight Zone, Texas.

Then there is the uncomfortably eerie case of the man who disappeared from a DC-3 as it flew from Kankakee, Illinois, to Dallas on June 29, 1968.

Jerrold L. Potter and his wife Carrie had been looking forward to attending the Lion's Club convention in Dallas for a long time. The fifty-four-year-old businessman was said to have been in good health, affable spirits, and secure in his financial concerns.

According to Emile Schurmacher's account in his *More Strange Unsolved Mysteries,* Potter got up to go to the lavatory somewhere over Texas airspace. His wife watched him start toward the compartment in the tail end of the aircraft. Several of Potter's friends had brief exchanges with him as he walked toward the lavatory.

Then the DC-3 gave an unaccountable jolt "as if it had bumped over an invisible obstacle in its flight path." The plane quivered a bit, then recovered almost at once. The passengers remained unconcerned by the unexpected turbulence.

After a few minutes, Mrs. Potter glanced down the aisle to see if her husband was returning to his seat. She became uneasy when he was nowhere in sight. She expressed her concern to a flight attendant, who checked the lavatory and found it empty.

Copilot Roy Bacus answered the stewardess' signal and was stunned to hear her report that a passenger was missing. He investigated the area of the rear lavatory and found that the boarding door was ajar. Bacus rushed forward to pilot Miguel Cabeza with a small section of the boarding door's safety chain. Cabeza radioed that he was changing his course, indicated the nature of the emergency, and headed for the nearest airport.

Investigating authorities found it difficult to accept the theory that Potter had mistakenly opened the exit door instead of the lavatory door. The exit door bore a warning inscription in large white letters on a red background. The door was hinged at the top and was secured by a safety chain and a heavy handle that could only be released by turning it 180 degrees to free two thick plunger bolts. It seemed totally unlikely that Potter could have thought it could be that difficult and complicated to open a lavatory door.

Grove Webster, president of Purdue Aviation Corporation, commented that it took a concentrated effort to open the exit door, and that it would have been extremely difficult to have done so during flight. "Although the DC-3 is not pressurized and a door could be opened without everyone being sucked out, it takes a lot of effort to open an exit door. Crews close the door for our stewardesses and open it," he explained. "And it is much harder to open and close in flight than on the ground."

There were twenty-two passengers and two flight attendants in the cabin when Potter disappeared, yet no one saw the businessman force open a door and plummet to his death. In fact, no one could recall seeing him after the DC-3 hit that "bump" in midair. Could Potter have had the misfortune to have been in precisely the proper position for an entrance into Texas' own Twilight Zone?

And apparently "things" also walk out of those same mysterious unseen boundaries.

On the evening of February 27, 1971, thirty-five-year-old Donald Childs of Lawton, Texas, suffered a heart attack when he looked out

in his front yard and saw a "wolfman" on its hands and knees attempting to drink out of an empty fishpond.

When he was released from the hospital two days later, Childs told police officer Clancy Williams that the creature had been "tall, with a lot of hair all over his face ... he was dressed in an indescribable manner."

Childs was not alone in his sighting of the werewolf. Other witnesses who viewed the incredible creature said that it was wearing pants "which were far too small for him."

The first reports of the wolfman came from west Lawton. Police officer Harry Ezell said that they received calls describing "something" running down the street, dodging cars, hiding behind bushes, then getting up and running again.

And while the skeptical might joke that the witnesses might very well have seen a very hairy hippie or a particularly hirsute vagrant, the physical feats that some observers described would have made the "hippie" a veritable superman.

Officer Ezell stated that police received a call from a man who had seen the monster sitting on a railing outside of his apartment.

"He told me he saw the thing when he opened the window curtain at about eleven-fifteen P.M.," Officer Ezell said. "He thought it was all a practical joke because the subject was perched on the railing. It looked like some big monkey or ape. He thought it was a joke until it turned its head and looked at him, then jumped off its perch on the second floor railing onto the ground seventeen feet below.

"The witness told me that the thing ran from the area on all fours, something like an ape would," Ezell continued. "The witness described it as wearing only pants which covered his leg to near his knee, as if it had outgrown the pants.

"He said that the thing had a horribly distorted face, as if it had been in a fire. It had hair all over its face, the upper parts of the body, and the lower parts of its legs."

A group of soldiers from Fort Still encountered the monster fifteen minutes later, and they freely admitted that the thing had frightened them.

The wolfman was sighted on Friday and Saturday nights in Lawton. Sunday night was quiet, and on Monday night, Major Clarence Hill, commander of the police patrol division, sent out an alert to be on careful watch for the "wolfman."

But by then the nightmarish creature, whatever it might have been, had already moved back into the Texas Twilight Zone from which it had come—unless that bizarre dimension of reality opens up again under an old farmhouse near Fouke, Arkansas.

Bobby Ford, twenty-five, moved into the old Crank place on May 1, 1971. He had lived in the house for less than five days when he had a face-to-face encounter with a six-foot-tall hairy monster. Ford said the creature had frightened him so badly that he had run "right through the front door—without opening it!"

# CHAPTER SEVEN

# THE STRANGE CASE OF CALIFORNIA'S TRAVELING DEAD MAN AND BITTER BIERCE'S HOLES IN TIME AND SPACE

The strange disappearance of Thomas P. Meehan, a thirty-eight-year-old Concord, California, attorney and referee for the state Department of Employment Appeals Bureau, would seem to suggest that there are certain places in which a bizarre kind of distortion of time and space occurs.

On February 1, 1963, Meehan left Eureka, California, for Concord at about 2:00 P.M. He drove as far as Myers Flat before he stopped to telephone his wife to report that he felt ill. She told him to spend the night at a motel and not try to drive straight through to their home.

From this point on the time sequence becomes most confusing—all the more so when the startling climax of the day's events is realized.

Approximately 5:00 P.M.: Meehan checked into the Forty Winks Motel at Redway.

Approximately 6:00 P.M.: The attorney drove to the Southern Humboldt Community Hospital at Garberville to see a doctor.

6:45 P.M.: Meehan told the nurse he felt as if he were dead.

Approximately 6:50 P.M.: Meehan disappeared while the nurse was checking him in and before he had seen a doctor.

Approximately 7:00 P.M.: A Myers Flat couple told the Highway Patrol that they had seen the taillights of a car on Highway 101 skid into the Eel River.

8:00 P.M.: Attorney Meehan was talking with Chip Nunnemaker, owner of the Forty Winks, at the motel. Nunnemaker recalled that Meehan kept asking him if he looked as though he were dead.

"He kept asking over and over, 'Do I look to you like I'm dead?'" the motel owner stated. "Meehan said, 'I feel like I've died, and the whole world died with me.'" Nunnemaker noticed that Meehan's shoes and trouser cuffs were wet and muddy.

9:00 P.M.: Meehan went to his room after having conversed with Nunnemaker for an hour.

9:30 P.M.: Motel employee Harry Young went to Meehan's room to tell him that the call he had put through to Mrs. Meehan could not be completed because a storm had disrupted telephone service. Young saw that the attorney had changed into a black suit and a white tie.

10:45 P.M.: The Highway Patrol found Meehan's car submerged in the Eel River, its taillamps shining like beacons for the searchers. Skid marks indicated that the vehicle had gone off the highway at high speed. Officers found blood on the exposed roof of the car. The right front window of the car was open. Meehan was nowhere in sight, but droplets of blood and muddy footprints led up the bank for thirty feet—then vanished.

No trace of Thomas Meehan could be found.

Nineteen days later, sixteen miles downstream from where his car had veered into the river, Meehan's body was discovered near Myers Flat. Autopsy evidence suggested that the attorney had survived the crash with a superficial head wound, then, later, had died of drowning.

Did Thomas Meehan's illness and confused state of mind lead him to weave in and out of hospitals and motel rooms and, finally, into a cold and swirling river? Or did that same confused mind exert an influence on time and space themselves?

If Meehan's automobile went into the river at about 7:00 P.M.— and it must have, since no other automobiles were reported missing or were ever found in the river on that date—how did he appear back at the motel to chat for the hour 8:00 to 9:00 P.M. with the owner? Nunnemaker did take note of Meehan's muddy shoes

and trouser cuffs and his repeated complaint that he felt as if he were dead. Employee Harry Young saw Meehan at 9:30 P.M. and observed that he had changed out of his wet clothing. Had Nunnemaker and Young actually talked with the ghost of a dead man? Or were they perceiving the understandable confusion of a man somehow lost between time and space?

Although Meehan did not vanish without a trace forever, he certainly did disappear and reappear all during the evening of February 1, 1963; and after he was last seen in his motel room by Harry Young, Meehan was not seen again until his body was found on February 20.

Meehan's automobile was seen to plunge into the Eel River at about the time he was sitting in the hospital at Garberville waiting to see a doctor. He conversed with a nurse, then disappeared before he actually saw a physician.

The police found drops of blood and muddy footprints that led up the riverbank for thirty feet before they simply vanished. Could Meehan, in a dazed condition, have made his way back to the Forty Winks Motel?

For the time sequence to work, he would have had to be picked up by another motorist. And why would he not have mentioned the accident sometime during his hour conversation with Nunnemaker and the other employees and guests at the motel? Why would Meehan, an attorney, not have reported the accident to the Highway Patrol? And why did no one at the motel notice Meehan's bleeding skull?

Is it possible that after changing into a clean suit and shirt and speaking with Harry Young at 9:30 P.M. Thomas Meehan wandered out into the night, walked back to the scene of the accident, and, ill and confused, fell into the river to drown? Or did Thomas Meehan actually drown shortly after his automobile went into the Eel River at about 6:45 P.M.? Meehan's will to live may have projected an image of himself to the nurse, to Nunnemaker, to Young while his actual physical self struggled for survival in the cold waters of the Eel River.

This peculiar case recalls Ambrose Bierce's remarkable short

story entitled, "An Occurrence at Owl Creek Bridge." In this tale, a man sentenced to a wartime execution by hanging from the girders of a bridge is able to visualize the rope breaking and a daring escape from his captors all in the split-second of reality before the taut rope snaps his neck and snuffs out his life-spark.

Could the dying Thomas Meehan have somehow discovered the same relativity of time and space? And could his mind in an altered state of consciousness have manipulated manmade time in a manner that would confuse all those who insist on measuring the passage of time by the movements of a clock hand? Could the dying Thomas Meehan have wavered between dimensions of time, dimensions of being, and utilized the unfathomable power of mind to influence matter?

✦

In the San Francisco of the later 1880s, Ambrose Bierce (then a columnist for William Randolph Hearst's *Sunday Examiner*) was the undisputed literary arbiter of the West Coast. Famous as a witty satirist, journalist, and short story writer (and later for his collection of cynical definitions, *The Devil's Dictionary*), he was fascinated by accounts of mysterious disappearances, reports of men and women who had vanished without a trace. Bierce himself disappeared under mysterious circumstances in late 1913 or early 1914.

Bierce was fond of quoting the theories of a Dr. Hern of Leipzig as explanations for the subject of strange disappearances. According to Bierce, Dr. Hern held that space was non-Euclidean, "that is to say, space has more dimensions than length, breadth, and thickness." Dr. Hern further believed that in the visible world we call reality there exist void places, *vacua*—"holes, as it were, through which animate and inanimate objects may fall into the invisible world and be seen and heard no more."

Dr. Hern viewed space as being pervaded by "luminiferous ether, which is a material thing—as much a substance as air or water, though almost infinitely more attenuated." The scientist postulated that "all force, all forms of energy must be propagated in this; every process must take place in it which takes place at all."

Bierce's own theory was that if such cavities should exist in this otherwise universal medium, as caverns exist in the earth or holes in Swiss cheese, an individual who had the misfortune to fall into such a cavity would be trapped in a voidlike dimension free of time and space as we understand it in our linear world. On occasion, perhaps, one might be able to walk through connected cavities as if the linkup formed a kind of tunnel through the third-dimensional parameters of time and space. Most often, however, the hapless victim would be suspended in a kind of limbo of the lost.

The question remains as to whether Ambrose Bierce himself was the victim of such a void or deliberately devised a method whereby it might simply appear as though he had vanished in the twinkling of an eye. One of Bierce's biographers, Franklin Walker, suggests that "The Wickedest Man in San Francisco" may have become so intrigued by the prospect of men and women vanishing without a trace that he set about planning his own enigmatic death. Walker feels that such a morbid joke would have appealed to Ambrose Bierce, who kept a human skull before him as he worked at his desk. Bierce may have reasoned that although physical death would one day be inescapable, he would be able to escape its normal attributes. He would cheat the undertaker, the biographer, and the public by disappearing without a trace.

In any event, Bierce was not snatched from "the midst of life" in midcareer or at the peak of his productive powers. He was seventy-one years old and suffered from asthmatic attacks intensified by sleeping off the effects of Demon Rum on a tombstone in a chilly San Francisco graveyard.

Bierce had been an extremely handsome younger man. He stood six feet tall, had reddish-blond flowing hair, and a full beard. Several biographers have made much of his "animal magnetism," which one states young women asserted they could feel when he stood ten feet away. Coupled with his striking good looks, Bierce was obsessed with cleanliness and attractive clothing. A seventy-one-year-old man perhaps no longer desired the pressures and mental tensions inherent in joining the ranks of the once beautiful.

50

Furthermore, Bierce's finest hours had been during the Civil War, in which he rose from drummer boy to first lieutenant and survived the bloody battles of Shiloh, Chickamauga, Murfreesboro, Kennesaw Mountain, Franklin, and Nashville, to be discharged brevet major.

But the war took its physical toll of Bierce. He was wounded twice, once seriously in the head. His brother felt that Ambrose was never the same after his head wound: "Some of the iron of the shell seemed to stick to his brain and he became bitter and suspicious." But it also hastened Ambrose's maturity from an Ohio farmboy to an intellectually mature man, eager to be a writer.

In spite of his magnetism, Bierce failed with women so often that he became an earnest misogynist. All the ingredients were there: He was handsome, virile, and strongly attracted to the opposite sex. But he worshiped women too much. He idealized women and tried in vain to place them upon a pedestal. When he discovered that they were creatures of flesh and blood with idiosyncrasies and failings, he grew disillusioned and even more bitter. His tirades against women were filled with his harshest invective—and their vehemence increased after he had destroyed his marriage to San Francisco society belle Ellen Day.

Bierce was, however, married long enough to father two sons and one daughter. He never stopped hating his wife for having failed him, and he loathed his sons for behaving as though they had come from a broken home. One son died of alcoholism at an early age, and the other was killed in a knife fight during a saloon brawl.

Somehow, in spite of his sour view of women, Bierce maintained a long and voluminous correspondence with both his daughter and his secretary, Carrie Christiansen.

Through all of his domestic difficulties, his struggles to establish himself as a writer, and his petulant sniping at his employer William Randolph Hearst, Bierce continually kindled his memories of the Civil War. At seventy, he decided to retrace his paths on the old Civil War battlefields and then to go to Mexico, where the counterrevolutionary forces led by Carranza and Villa had risen

against the federal troops of President Victoriano Huerta.

In his final letter from Laredo, Texas, dated December 16, 1913, Bierce declared to Carrie Christiansen that he was crossing the border into Mexico "with a pretty definite purpose which is not at present disclosable."

Although that is the last word Ambrose Bierce is known to have set to paper before his mysterious disappearance, a certain amount of substantial evidence indicates that the old warrior was seen alive after that date. Some accounts state that Bierce was killed in a campaign in January 1914. Others indicate that the author was executed by a firing squad, murdered by guides, or killed by soldiers who grew impatient with his stinging tongue.

Odo B. Slade, a onetime member of Pancho Villa's staff, recalled an elderly American with gray hair and an asthmatic condition who served as a military adviser to Villa. The American was called Jack Robinson, and he criticized Villa's battle strategies with the accomplishment of a military expert.

In his book *They Never Came Back,* Allen Churchill comments on the possibility of Bierce having served as Pancho Villa's adviser: "It is easy to picture the malevolent oldster parading his military knowledge before the Mexicans. It is also possible to relish him urging companions to call him by the boyishly adventurous name of Jack Robinson."

Slade and author Louis Stevens (in *Here Comes Pancho Villa!*) both state that this "Jack Robinson" quarreled violently with Villa and was shot to death when he announced his intention to leave and transfer his allegiance to Carranza.

Other investigators have also theorized that the clever Bierce never really crossed the Mexican border at all, but remained hidden in the United States to die in obscurity and have a last laugh at all those who puzzled over his mysterious disappearance.

And then, there are those who insist that Bierce himself may have toppled into a hole in space "through which animate and inanimate objects may fall into the invisible world and be seen and heard no more."

# CHAPTER EIGHT

# THE VISION THAT SAVED A SCALPING VICTIM'S LIFE

The ordeal of scalping victim Josiah Wilbarger has become a classic frontier tale, somewhat akin to John Colter's race for life and other stories of mountain men and frontiersmen who survived what appeared to be certain death. Although the account has now been told in a number of books and periodicals, it has been a favorite of ours since we first heard it over thirty years ago, and we were eager to retell the tale in our own style. Josiah's vision has secured a place in this present collection because of its account of a remarkable paranormal linkup between the wounded man and his sister.

Josiah Wilbarger stood in the stirrups and squinted into the hot Texas sun of an August afternoon in 1833. "Near as I can tell," he said to his four companions, "we be about eight miles from Reuben Hornsby's place."

William Strother pointed toward a clump of trees off to the right of the trail. "Then let's stop to water our horses at the spring. Eight miles is too far to push these beasts in this infernal heat."

With low grunts of ready agreement, the five men reined their mounts toward the spring—a mistake two of them would not live to regret.

Rifle-armed Comanches opened fire on them before the Texans

even had a chance to dismount. Hidden by the clump of trees, the Comanches had watched the five frontiersmen approach the spring as if they were being delivered into their hands by the Great Mystery.

Josiah Wilbarger, struck by a rifle ball at the base of his skull, toppled from his saddle. Thomas Christian and William Strother were also knocked off their horses by the Comanches' volley. The two remaining men in the party wheeled their mounts and pounded leather, riding for their lives.

Josiah Wilbarger lay stunned in the tall grasses near the spring. In 1833, Comanche warriors were far more proficient with bows and arrows than with rifles, and the brave who had shot him had measured an inadequate powder charge. Properly primed and loaded, a rifle ball that caught a man at the base of the skull would have taken half the victim's head off. Josiah lay bleeding and dazed, but he was very much alive. Alive enough to know that if he wanted to stay that way, he had better play dead.

Josiah heard the screams and groans of Christian and Strother as Comanche braves cut their throats. Mercifully, he felt himself sliding back into unconsciousness as a knee slammed roughly into his lower back and powerful fingers jerked his head up by his hair. As if in a nightmare, Josiah felt the smooth fire of the brave's knife as it sliced a crude circle in his scalp. Because of the open wound at the base of his skull, the Comanche who had shot him had assumed that the frontiersman was already quite dead. Without further ceremony, the brave was helping himself to Josiah's scalp.

It was nearly dark when the Texan recovered consciousness. The Comanches had left him naked, stripped of all his clothing and personal possessions. Blood had matted one eye shut, but through the other he could make out the forms of his slain companions.

Somehow, Josiah managed to get his elbows beneath him and started to crawl. Reuben Hornsby's cabin was eight miles away. Maybe, with God's help, he could make it.

After what seemed an eternity of crawling, his torn and bleeding hands touched the rough bark of a tree. Struggling to assume an upright, sitting position, he leaned against the trunk and fought to control his ragged breathing.

"It is here I'll die," he decreed solemnly to the darkness. "Here, beneath this tree, I'll join my Maker."

"*Nonsense, Josiah Wilbarger*," scolded the soft female voice. "*You always were the great one for exaggeration.*"

Josiah blinked his eyes in disbelief as he slowly raised his head and saw the form of his sister Margaret standing before him. She had her hands on her hips, and her lips were pursed. She was frowning at him as if she were very impatient and angry with him but her eyes gave her away, as they always had. When they had been children and Margaret, as older sister, had been a second mother to the Wilbarger brood, her eyes had always sparkled their love regardless of how fierce she had tried to look when she reprimanded them.

"Margaret," he gasped, wishing somehow that he could cover his bloody nakedness. "Whatever are you doing here?"

"Looking after you, boy," she smiled, "as always. You've really fixed yourself this time, haven't you?"

"Aye," he nodded, then winced at the pain the movement of his head had brought him. "But I had the willing cooperation of a rifle-toting, knife-slicing Comanche to get me into this trouble."

"Well," Margaret sighed, and there was sadness in her eyes, "what's done is done. Now I can't be staying but another little bit, so I want you to listen to me and heed what I tell you. Do you understand me?"

Josiah whispered that he understood his elder sister, but the simple truth was that his throbbing brain was too pain-loaded to have any desire to attempt to sort out the mystery of how his sister had come to be in the middle of a Texas plain when she lived on the home place back in Kentucky.

"Mind that you stay right under this tree, Josiah," Margaret was telling him. "It'll give you shade from the sun and serve as a landmark for those lads who are coming to rescue you. Now it is important that you stay here, boy, because there'll be someone along for you before sunset tomorrow night. Josiah, you must stay here beneath this tree. Do you understand me?"

"Yes, Margaret," Josiah mumbled, his head dropping to his chest

as he swooned with pain.

He did not awaken again until morning. His lips were parched with thirst, and his skull seemed to be the entire painful essence of his being. It was as if he had no arms or legs or body. He was only a throbbing skull that moaned its hurt on a Texas plain.

Then, in a moment when the pain subsided enough to permit him to think of survival, he decided that he must crawl on. His only hope lay in reaching the Hornsby cabin.

In the next moment of clarity, he remembered Margaret. How real she had seemed last night. He could have reached out and touched her if he had had the strength. What was it she had said? *"Stay under the tree, Josiah!"*

She had always given him good advice when he was a boy. Perhaps he should listen to her now. Besides, he sighed, leaning back against the trunk of the tree, he doubted if he had the strength to crawl much farther.

✤

Throughout the day Josiah had terrible hallucinations. The Comanches had come back for him. With whoops of sadistic glee, the painted braves unsheathed their knives and moved in on him. At the last moment they changed to buzzards with hungry beaks and mottled, flapping black wings.

About an hour before sunset Josiah felt himself being lifted gently into a buckboard. A canteen sloshed water against his parched lips, and he allowed the liquid to trickle into his mouth.

Then he was grabbing wildly for the canteen, moaning his terrible thirst.

"Easy, lad," a voice told him. "Don't gulp it at first. Plenty of time for drinkin' later."

"Reuben," Josiah managed in a hoarse whisper. "Is it you, man? How did you find me? How did you know I was here?"

"You never mind about that now," Hornsby told him. "The important thing is that we did find you."

Josiah did not receive the complete story of his miraculous rescue until nearly a week later. Then, one night when he was able to

sit up and enjoy an after-dinner pipe with his host, he was told the strange circumstances under which Hornsby and his neighbors had known where to look for him.

Mrs. Hornsby had awakened from a dream and had prodded Reuben out of his own sound sleep. She insisted that she had seen Josiah, naked and bloody, propped up under a large tree about eight miles from their cabin. Reuben hushed his wife for troubling him with her nightmares, but she was so insistent that the following morning he contacted a number of his neighbors and they went in search of Josiah Wilbarger.

The mystery did not end with Mrs. Hornsby's truth-telling dream, which had led to the rescue of the badly wounded Josiah— or with Josiah's own peculiar vision of his sister, who had instructed him to remain at the tree so that rescuers might find him.

A month later, Josiah Wilbarger received a letter notifying him that his beloved sister Margaret had died in her sleep at her home in Kentucky at the precise hour at which she had appeared to him under the tree on the prairie.

# CHAPTER NINE

# THE DEVIL RIDER OF CHISHOLM HOLLOW

O n a warm summer's day in 1846 Bert McConnell paused before the hollow to prime his double-barreled shotgun. A hardworking rancher, McConnell had had enough of going out in the mornings to find his cattle torn up by a pack of marauding wolves. For two days he and one of his ranch hands had tracked the howling beasts, and now he figured for certain they had found the wolves' lair in the wooded hollow that lay before them.

"We aren't going to go in there, are we, sir?"

McConnell was startled by Mike MacCarty's question. "Are you thinkin' that we would just whistle for them like sheepdogs and the bloody creatures will come walkin' out for us to shoot away at them?"

MacCarty shifted anxiously in his saddle. "Well, sir, I was truly thinking that maybe we would wait until nightfall and shoot the pack as it came howling out of the hollow."

"By the saints, man," McConnell felt his temper rising, "we've already lost a full day of work tracking the beasts. I cannot see my way clear to wasting two more hours 'til nightfall. Besides, it's best to get them in their lair before they start to move about."

MacCarty cleared his throat nervously. "How would it be, sir, if you went into the hollow and flushed them out, and I stayed here to be certain none of the bloody things get away?"

McConnell could not believe his ears. Mike was one of his best hands and had served him well for nearly seven years now. "Michael, me boy, is it that you are somehow afraid to go into the hollow?"

MacCarty could not meet his boss' angry stare, and he fixed his eyes on his horse's reins as he answered. "Well, you must know that no Indian will go into that hollow. And not many white men will venture within, neither."

McConnell rolled his eyes impatiently skyward. "Is it that talk about the old Spanish ghost that has got you spooked, man? I cannot believe what I am hearing."

McConnell's family had been ranching in the central Texas hill country for nearly thirty years. Both he and his father had fought in the Texas War for Independence back in '36. The first settlers in the region had been Scots-Irish hillmen who had migrated mostly from the states of Kentucky and Tennessee. God-fearing though they were, a vein of superstition and a healthy respect for the supernatural ran through their heritage. When some old Indians had told the ranchers to avoid a small valley because of an evil spirit on horseback, a good many of the superstitious hillmen had decided that there was enough land in Texas without trespassing on haunted ground. McConnell knew that many of his fellow ranchers gave the hollow a wide berth.

"Mike," he growled at his hand, "I've got both barrels of this here scattergun loaded with buckshot. One blast of this will stop any h'ant there is."

"But, Mr. McConnell, sir," Mike protested. "I, myself, have heard some weird clankin' noises coming from that hollow."

"I'm gonna clank you alongside the head if you don't come with me right now, boy!"

Without further discussion, MacCarty followed his boss down into the draw that led into the hollow. After going about a hundred yards, he dismounted and bent near the ground to examine some confused animal tracks they had discovered.

"What you make of them?" McConnell wanted to know.

Just then the sharp clanking of metal on metal and the thudding

of hooves caused both men to turn their heads. They would argue for years to come over which of them was the most astounded to see the armored rider on the big black horse thundering down on them. MacCarty jumped back on his own horse, and both of the cattlemen galloped out of the hollow as quickly as their mounts could manage the retreat.

Shortly after the incident, of which McConnell and MacCarty made no secret, the people of the hill country learned that the army of General Zachary Taylor had crossed the Rio Grande and had violated Mexican territory. The Mexican War had begun.

The Devil Rider of Chisholm Hollow is a strange manifestation that the people of the central Texas hills have claimed to have seen before every major conflict in which the United States has become embroiled. The strikingly tall, armored horseman on his magnificent coal-black steed is seen to thunder out of the little valley, then vanish without a trace.

The second recorded manifestation of the rider was fifteen years after he had terrified Bert McConnell and his ranch hand. The report was given by Emmett Ringstaff, and this time the Devil Rider was described more completely.

On April 10, 1861, Ringstaff happened to be passing the hollow when the rider came by him at a steady trot. The horse the phantom rode was taller than any that had been raised by the settlers of the area, and even though the hill folk thought the rider to be a manifestation of Lucifer, Ringstaff remained calm enough to observe that the specter was wearing a kind of armor and carrying a shield. Iron gauntlets covered his arms, and he wore a helmet of Spanish design. From a buckler, which looked to be gold and bore an inscription of a crown and a lion, two brass pistols dangled. The weapons were of eighteenth-century design and had the look of fine craftsmanship about them.

Shortly after Ringstaff saw the apparition of the phantom horseman, the first guns of the Civil War were fired at Fort Sumter.

After the War Between the States had ended, the hollow was christened Chisholm Hollow because of its geographic location on a spur of the Chisholm Trail, one of the principal trails Texas ranchers used to drive their stock to Kansas railheads. The Devil Rider never seemed to bother the cattlemen, and on one occasion a couple of bold cowboys picked up a few interesting artifacts out of the hollow, including a large silver spur of old Spanish design.

Still later, the settlers learned from historians that a Spanish fort had been located near the hollow when Texas had been under Spain's control. According to some recordkeepers, the garrison that had been stationed near the fort had been massacred by Comanches around 1700.

Gradually the notion that the phantom rider was a manifestation of the Devil gave way to the theory that he was the ghost of one of the Spanish soldiers who had been killed in the massacre of nearly two centuries before.

Before the Spanish-American war, the mysterious rider in armor was seen by three men: Arch Clawson, Ed Shannon, and Sam Bulluck. Although the pattern of the ghostly figure's visitation had not changed, a new twist had been added. Each one of the men who saw the rider felt, at that particular instant, an eerie flash of animosity that the phantom was directing personally at him. Each of the witnesses felt as though the spirit had come close to drawing one of his spectral pistols and putting a ball through him.

After the Spanish-American war broke out, area residents theorized that they had a reason for the Devil Rider's apparent hostility toward the witnesses who had perceived his materialization. The ghost was sensitive about his Spanish heritage. Though the strange horseman had remained neutral when portending other conflicts, this time his loyalty lay with Spain, and his prejudice seemed to manifest itself in overt ways.

All during the brief conflict with the Spanish, strange things hap-

pened around the central Texas hills. Though the rest of the state had a better-than-average rainfall in 1898, wells and creeks went dry in the hill country. Cattle died of thirst, and an unexplainable disease began killing the horses. These local calamities are still blamed on the Devil Rider by the folklore of the people who live in the area of the hollow.

Only one attempt was ever made to settle in the hollow, and that was unsuccessful. Scoffing at the superstitions of the small ranching community, the homesteader began building a house so he could claim rights on the land in the hollow. He had just completed the task of erecting a home when the entire building unexplainably burst into flames. All that has remained of the attempted invasion of the Devil Rider's hollow is a crumbling chimney.

After the phantom rider's appearance before the Spanish-American war, the apparition kept to itself in the secluded hollow. He would not be seen again until January of 1917 when he materialized for a group of young deer hunters who had decided to tempt the fates and look for deer signs within the hollow.

Old-timers long recalled how the three bold young men had laughed at the wild tales and superstitions of their elders. They were modern folks, two of them with high school educations; they would not be kept away from bagging some good venison by ghost stories of devil riders.

Glancing over their shoulders just the same, they had entered the hollow very cautiously. And just like all the brave and bold scoffers before them, the three deer hunters scattered and ran when the armored rider suddenly appeared out of nowhere, his armor and mail glinting in the winter sun.

On February 3, 1917, the United States, which had been teetering on the brink of war, severed diplomatic relations with the German Empire, and shortly after was sending Yanks across the Atlantic to France.

In 1941, the world was turning upside down. Europe had been a battlefield for a year and a half, and the Western Pacific had been subject to Japanese aggression for even longer. Not insensitive to the precarious position of the United States in such a troubled world setting, many of the people of the central hills of Texas had gathered to pray for peace on Sunday, December 7.

Following the services, two couples got into an automobile and started down the road that led to Chisholm Hollow. As they passed the haunted valley, the driver stopped the car, insisting that he had heard a horse.

After a few seconds, the mounted apparition of the armored Spanish soldier charged onto the road, stopped broadside to the two couples for an instant, then passed on and disappeared in the cover on the opposite side of the trail.

The terrified men and women hurried to the home of one of the couples, where they sat anxiously around the radio and waited impatiently for the tubes to warm up. The first words they heard were of the bombing of Pearl Harbor.

Sober and sincere witnesses have declared that they saw the Devil Rider appear just prior to the conflicts in Korea and Vietnam.

"He seemed to miss Desert Storm, though," said one student of the phenomenon. "The old Devil Rider must have known that war was going to be a quick one."

# CHAPTER TEN

# The Haunt of Bailey's Prairie
# and the Spook Light of
# Chinati Mountain

**B**rit Bailey's dying request was that he be buried standing upright.

"I spent my whole life stomping over these here prairies," he gasped, "and I don't aim to stop walking 'em when I die."

They buried old Brit in 1833, but residents in the area of Bailey's Prairie still claim today that the early settler has kept his promise about stomping around on the prairies that lie five miles west of Angleton, Texas, in Brazoria County.

The Thomas family, who moved into old Brit's place after he had been planted erect in the sod according to his wishes, soon bore witness that the old-timer's ghost did not wait long to start prowling around.

In her diary, Ann Rainey Thomas recorded her sighting of old Brit when the apparition looked in the window one night.

The Thomas' servant girl, Melinda, said that the ghost chased the menservants away from the cows one evening at milking time.

Eventually, all the members of the Thomas household swore to having heard old Brit's shuffling footsteps moving around the house after dark. Once when Mr. Thomas lay ill, he claimed that he clearly saw Brit Bailey in the room with him.

Not until the early 1850s, however, did Bailey's spook light begin to be seen on the prairie. Colonel Mordello Munson and several of

his guests saw a weirdly glowing ball of light drift slowly past his home early one evening. Saddling their horses, the colonel and the male guests gave the eerie globe a hardy pursuit but were unable to capture it or clearly identify it.

From that night on, Brit Bailey's Light has drifted across the Texas prairieland the old settler was so reluctant to relinquish. Even today, area residents claim to see it.

❖

Since pioneer days, night travelers in the area of Chinati Mountain in the Cienagas Range of southwestern Texas have witnessed a most unusual phenomenon. An odd, peculiarly glowing ball—about the size of a modern basketball—materializes, moves about, splits into twin spheres, re-forms, and runs a range of intensity varying from a more twinkle to a blinding glare.

According to area residents, the best spot for observing the spook light is along Highway 90 between Marfa and Alpine. As to a "rational" explanation for the mysterious light, residents, investigating scientists, and other eyewitnesses have been embroiled in fiery controversy for generations.

Those who emphasize the word *spook* when they talk of the strange light refer to the legend of the ancient Apache chief Alsate to explain the source of the glowing orb. It seems that Alsate was tricked into offending a tribal deity after he had been betrayed by some fast-talking Mexicans in the early 1800s. As his eternal punishment, Alsate was condemned to wander the Big Bend country of Texas. It is the old Apache's spirit that one sees when witnessing a manifestation of the spook light.

Other theories attribute the source of the ghost light to the reflection of moonlight on deposits of mica in the cliffs and crags of the mountains. This, however, does not explain the brightly glowing ball on nights when the moon is hidden by thick cloud banks.

Some residents maintain that the spook light is seen under only two conditions: either just before or just after a rain. But Dr. John Dismant, professor of geology at Sul Ross State College, argues

that he has seen the light "dozens of times when the country was bone-dry!"

For those who are stumped because the ghost light shines on nights when the moon does not, some clever citizens came up with the theory that the mysterious illumination was caused by the reflection of automobile headlights coming down Paisana Pass.

But how does the spook light maintain a steady glow of several hours' duration if it has to depend on the headlights of an occasional automobile that may speed by rather quickly? And what about the fact that the earliest settlers and travelers in southwestern Texas mentioned seeing the ghost light? Covered wagons and stagecoaches did not come equipped with powerful headlights.

Whether the engimatic light of Chinati Mountain is caused by certain unique climatic conditions working on mineral deposits peculiar to that area or whether observers are really seeing the glowing spirit of Chief Alsate, one indisputable fact remains. The spook light is there.

# CHAPTER ELEVEN

# SILVER CLIFF'S GHOSTLY MINERS

The group of miners had just finished celebrating Clyde McCollough's birthday, old Ben Murchison's new pair of eyeglasses, Charlie Benthurst's new belt buckle—and anything else that they could think of on that merry night in 1880. They were still laughing and making foolish toasts to whatever came to mind when they passed the Silver Cliff cemetery.

"Do you boys believe in ghosts?" Charlie Benthurst asked his jovial companions.

"Charlie's right," old Ben roared agreement. "Let's drink a toast to a ghost!"

"No, no." Charlie was stammering now. His bottle fell from his hand and broke when it struck a rock in the rough road on which they walked. "L-look at the cemetery! There are ghosts m-moving around!"

When the group of miners saw the flickering blue lights bobbing over the gravestones, they swallowed their laughter in sober gulps and left the area in a big hurry.

✤

Since that night in 1880, the ghost lights have been observed in the old miners' cemetery by several generations of tourists and residents of Silver Cliff, Colorado, located in the Wet Mountain Valley.

Today, with few more than a hundred inhabitants, Silver Cliff itself is little more than a ghost town, but in 1880 it was a bustling mining community of 5,087.

Word of the ghost lights first reached the media in the spring of 1956 in the *Wet Mountain Tribune*. Then, on August 20, 1967, the spooky cemetery became national news when an account of the ghost lights appeared in *The New York Times*.

Several witnesses have observed that the curious blue lights cannot be seen as clearly on the sandstone graveyard markers as on the wooden crosses. Such an observation has convinced a number of theorists that the lights are only reflections of houselights in the city.

County Judge August Menzel said that he could readily counter that theory. He remembered the night when everyone in Silver Cliff and in nearby Westcliff deliberately agreed to shut off their lights. Even the streetlights were turned off, "But the graveyard lights still danced."

✜

In the August 1969 issue of *National Geographic*, Edward J. Linehan, the magazine's assistant editor, wrote of his observation of the Silver Cliff ghost lights.

Linehan drove to the old cemetery in the company of Bill Kleine, proprietor of the local campground. It was a cloudy night, and after they had bounced about a mile across the prairie outside Silver Cliff, Kleine told the journalist to shut off his headlights. The two men climbed out of the car, standing for a few moments in silence.

"There!" Kleine directed in an urgent whisper. "See them there? And over there?"

Linehan saw them—"dim, round spots of blue-white light" glowing ethereally among the graves. He spotted another, closer at hand. He stepped forward for a better look and the lights vanished.

The two men walked about the cemetery for fifteen minutes, pursuing one ghost light, then another. Linehan aimed his flashlight at one spook light and snapped it on only to reveal a tombstone caught in its beam.

Kleine told Linehan that some people believed that the lights

were due to phosphorescence caused by decaying wood in the crosses. Others dismissed the ghost lights as reflections from the town lights of Silver Cliff or Westcliff.

Linehan looked at the two small Western towns in the distance. The tiny clusters of lights seemed much too faint to be able to be reflected way out there in the cemetery.

"The trouble with that theory is that my wife and I have both seen these lights when the fog was so thick that you couldn't see either one of these towns at all," Kleine said.

Many of the old-timers in the area look with amusement upon efforts to explain away the ghost lights as some phenomenon due to unknown but natural causes. According to these elderly men and women and the legend they still repeat, the old cemetery came to be the final resting place for many miners who died while scraping precious ores out of the mountain valley. The flickering globes of the graveyard ghost lights resemble, so say the old-timers, the little lights that used to be worn on the miners' caps; and legend has it that the eerie lights are actually the restless souls of the miners who still search for the bonanza they never found in life.

If the ghostly graveyard lights cannot be attributed to the reflection of ordinary house and municipal lights, just what can they be? Amateur and professional researchers alike have come up with several explanations:

1. The ghost lights are reflections from the stars overhead. (But the lights are just as clearly seen on starless, moonless nights.)

2. The graveyard lights are caused by radioactive ores. (But Geiger counters used to cover the entire area have revealed no trace of radioactivity.)

3. The mysterious lights are merely reflections of the mercury vapor of the Westcliff streetlights. (But during a Westcliff power failure the eerie graveyard lights remained undimmed; besides, there were no mercury-vapor streetlights in 1880.)

4. Hoaxsters with luminous paint are responsible for the ghost lights. (But no evidence has ever been found to support such a charge, from 1880 to modern times.)

Even the most persistent seekers of a plausible explanation for the Silver Cliff mystery lights have been forced to admit their total bafflement. To add to every theorist's confusion, the ghost lights cannot be approached for a closer examination. As soon as anyone comes too near, the spook lights seem to disappear—only to pop up again in another section of the cemetery. Photographers have been hired to capture the elusive lights on film, but none of the camera technicians has been very successful in obtaining a clear image of the mysterious blue lights.

If the mystery lights of Silver Cliff cemetery are truly the illuminated souls of frustrated miners, then they certainly provide us with a dandy ghost story devoid of any elements of subjective emotionality and offer an ever-present proof for the most skeptical doubter of such phenomena. Until someone someday supplies irrefutable evidence to the contrary, romanticists will probably cherish the ghost-story potential of the Silver Cliff cemetery.

As Edward Linehan concluded his article in *National Geographic*: "No doubt someone, someday, will prove there's nothing at all supernatural in the luminous manifestations of Silver Cliff's cemetery. And I will feel a tinge of disappointment. I prefer to believe [the spook lights] are the restless stirrings of the ghosts of Colorado, eager to get their state on with its pressing business: seeking out and working the bonanzas of a second glorious century."

# CHAPTER TWELVE

# THE ANGEL AND THE LAWMAN WHO CLEANED UP TOMBSTONE

The moment one starts talking about the lawman who cleaned up Tombstone Territory, the average Western buff, educated almost solely by motion pictures and television, will immediately visualize the image of Wyatt Earp as portrayed by Henry Fonda, Hugh O'Brien, or Burt Lancaster. Contrary to dozens of cinematic impersonations, Earp was really more of a gambler and a cardsharp than he was a lawman. And he was never marshal of Tombstone or any other frontier town.

Television fans of O'Brien's highly sanitized interpretation of "Deacon Wyatt" would be shocked to learn that the real Earp was not above slapping women around to keep them in line. In 1877 when he was dealing a game of faro in a Dodge City saloon, he beat up a dancehall girl named Frankie Bell. He was fined one dollar for disturbing the peace, and Frankie was fined twenty dollars for having cursed Earp while he was slapping her.,

But Earp was really master of the six-shooter, right? Well, he set off a stampede of panic in the Custom House Saloon in Wichita when, as he sat playing cards, his revolver accidentally fell out of its holster. Although it was customary to keep only five cartridges in your sixgun, allowing the hammer to rest on an empty chamber for safety's sake, Earp apparently did not practice such caution. The revolver discharged as it struck the floor and the slug passed

through Earp's coat, struck the north wall of the saloon, then glanced off and passed out through the ceiling.

When Wyatt Earp, his brother, and his pal Doc Holliday left Tombstone after the famous gunfight at the OK Corral, the Arizona community was far from clean. If anything, crime was more rampant than before the Earp regime.

The fiction of Earp as the virtuous defender of law and order was largely the creation of Ned Buntline, a prolific dime-novel writer. The man who actually pinned on a tin star and really mopped up the territory was Texas John Slaughter.

Slaughter had been a successful rancher in Texas before he moved to Arizona, so he was accustomed to rubbing up against some tough hombres. He was quick with his wits, fast on the draw with his pearl-handled revolver, and doggedly determined to make Tombstone a decent city.

Besides his courage and his stubbornness, Texas John had two important advantages over all the previous lawmen who had tried to tame Tombstone and had failed: a dependable sixth sense and an active guardian angel.

"I've got a guardian angel who protects me," he would tell well-meaning friends when they sought to caution him about his dangerous life-style. "I am completely serious when I say that my angel keeps those rough owlhoots and gunslicks from even denting me. I'll die in bed when I am good and ready—and when my guardian angel says that it's time to go."

The way Texas John explained it to his closest associates was that he heard a buzz inside his head whenever danger was near. He had long ago learned to recognize that sound as an alert that was transmitted to him by his guardian angel, and he did not question it whenever it went off. Texas John automatically drew his weapon and went on guard whenever he received the buzzing signal from his invisible protector.

Once, when Texas John was riding his famous big gray horse on his way to buy some cattle, he received the familiar warning buzz from his guardian angel that told him that he was approaching danger. He sat on his horse for quite a while, assessing the message

from his invisible guardian. His well-trained senses scanned the terrain before him, but he could neither see anything nor pick up any signs of threat. The problem was, whenever he started to ride forward, the buzz got louder and assured him that danger lay ahead.

Since Texas John never argued with the angelic warning signal, he decided to ride into the town of Tubac. He dismounted and went into one of his favorite general stores to visit a while with the owner, who also hailed from the Lone Star state. Texas John did not stop trading yarns with the storekeeper until his angel sent him the all-clear signal.

Later that day, three sun-parched gunslingers who worked for Texas John's archenemy, Curly Bill Brocius, rode into Tubac and headed straight for the saloon. Over beers they could be overheard cursing their bad luck. It seemed that Curly Bill had learned of Texas John Slaughter's cattle-buying trip and had sent the three of them to lie in ambush for him.

"We squatted out there in that boiling sun until we felt like venison being dried for the winter," one of them growled to a local tough.

"I got so dry and thirsty that I started belching dust," another of the owlhoots complained. "I know that Curly Bill is going to be mad and fit to fry us, but we ain't no damned Apaches. No white man could stay out there in that sun all day and not have his brains boiled."

The third hired gun added his gripe. "We waited long enough, that's for sure. We could have stayed under those mesquite bushes until Christmas waiting for Slaughter. Something just plain told him to go another way, that's all."

Although Texas John had his share of shootouts, he used a shotgun and a rifle more often than his revolver—and he never faced an outlaw in a dramatic duel on a dusty street at high noon. And

there seems no actual evidence that a Hollywood-style shootout with smoking revolvers ever took place in the real West—certainly not where any gunfighter truly killed or seriously wounded his opponent.

The mystique of the West has forever enshrined the Colt .44 "Peacemaker" as the traditional weapon of choice for every lawman and desperado who ever lived, but the shotgun was really the firearm that tamed the frontier. There is no question that a handgun was worn on a good many of the hips that went West, but when it came to a serious shootout, sheriffs, marshals, professional gunfighters, and even the awesome Texas Rangers relied on their scatterguns. The most direct plan of action in the typical gunfight in the Old West was to crouch behind rocks or trees and to ambush the adversary with a shotgun.

✛

One night Texas John and his wife had attended a social function at a neighbor's ranch and were driving home after dark in their buckboard. Mrs. Slaughter saw her husband cock his head in the bright moonlight, as if he were listening to a sound that she could not perceive.

"What do you hear, John?" she asked, trying to mask her nervousness.

Slaughter handed her the reins and reached for his double-barreled shotgun. "My angel just sent me the buzz," he told her in a soft but firm voice.

"Do you want me to take the reins?" she asked.

Texas John placed the shotgun across his knees and unholstered his revolver. "Yes," he nodded, handing her the reins. "I think we'll be a whole lot safer if you drive, and I have my six-gun in my hand."

The transfer of the buckboard's reins had scarcely been completed when a horseman emerged from the shadows, and the angry features of the notorious rustler Ike Clanton were distinguishable in the moonlight. The tough old patriarch of the outlaw clan had sworn on many occasions to kill the troublesome sheriff, and he

rode out in front of the Slaughters' buckboard with his revolver already drawn.

But when Ike saw the moonlight glinting off the six-gun in the fast-shooting Slaughter's hand, he turned his horse and rode on without speaking a word or firing a shot.

Texas John's ever-vigilant guardian angel got the lawman through a seemingly endless number of close scrapes and violent shootouts. Slaughter's incredible sixth sense never lost its effectiveness.

Many years later, when Tombstone, the Clantons, and Curly Bill had become the stuff of memoirs and memories, the old frontier sheriff found out that his guardian angel's interest in his physical welfare had not diminished with age.

On the evening of May 4, 1921, while Texas John sat in his dining room reading the evening paper, he got the buzz, the old danger signal, once again.

"It was as if I heard my faithful guardian angel actually screaming right in my ear," Slaughter said later. "Yes, there was a bit of the old buzz, but this time I heard my angel shout at me 'Get away from that open window and get your gun!'"

Startled but ever heedful of the invisible adviser, Slaughter set down his newspaper and sprang to his feet. He was in the bedroom buckling his gun when two shots rang out that killed his foreman, Jess Fisher.

When the four ranch hands involved in the plot were arrested by local police officers, they confessed that Slaughter was also to have been killed. One of the conspirators had been drawing a bead on Texas John, who sat reading his newspaper in front of an open window, when Slaughter suddenly jumped to his feet and moved quickly out of sight. Another instant longer over the newspaper and the old lawman, who made an easy target in the light from the reading lamp, would have been dead.

"What have I always told you?" Texas John said to his friends. "My guardian angel told me years ago that I would not die by bul-

let, knife, or accident. He said that I would die in my bed of natural causes. Once again, he sent me the warning in time so that that bushwhacker's bullet never found me. My angel has promised not to let anything happen to me until it is my time to go."

Texas John Horton Slaughter's time to go finally came in 1922 when he passed away in his own bed where he lay felled by a stroke. His guardian angel had kept his word and not allowed an enemy's weapon to harm the lawman who really cleaned up Tombstone Territory.

# CHAPTER THIRTEEN

# THE GHOST IN THE CALICO DRESS

They say that the ghost of Rebecca Dorrington walks at night in the 118-year-old hotel in the tiny High Sierra hamlet of Dorrington, California. The town itself was named for Rebecca, the Scottish bride of John Gardener, an 1850s homesteader who built the old hotel. Those residents of Dorrington who believe that the ghost still walks attribute the phenomenon to the violent manner in which Rebecca left this life.

Some say she froze to death in a blizzard. Others maintain that she was killed by Indians. Still other accounts of the legend insist that Rebecca fell down a flight of stairs and bled to death. Then, apart from these widely varied theories of Rebecca's tragic demise is the belief that she died from pneumonia sometime late in the 1860s or early in the 1870s.

However Rebecca made her transition from the earth plane, many contend that her restless spirit has not ceased to acquaint guests in the hotel with the force of her personality. According to accounts going back several years, the old hotel is the scene of such classic manifestations in the supernatural repertoire as doors banging open and shut, lights flashing on and off, and furniture being shifted.

One recent guest gives her credence to the theory that Rebecca Dorrington died after a cruel fall down a flight of stairs.

"I was awakened in the middle of the night by this terrible racket that sounded like someone falling tail-over-teakettle down the stairs," she said. "Thinking that someone had sustained a nasty fall, I came out to investigate and to see if I might be of help. As I approached the stairs, I clearly heard the sobs of a woman in pain, but when I got there, I could see absolutely no one in sight."

Ed Wilson, whose wife had been a great-granddaughter of Rebecca Dorrington, told the Los Angeles *Times* (October 31, 1969) that tales of the ghost were repeated only by "damn fools, drunks, and historians." But he conceded that "we never knew how Rebecca died."

Leonard Anderson, who owned the hotel from 1947 to 1960, admitted that the place is full of weird noises and strange squeaking sounds, but he feels that the villagers "use Rebecca's ghost to spice up the conversation whenever things become dull in Dorrington."

In spite of the numerous doubters, many villagers have sworn that they've met the restless spirit of Rebecca Dorrington wearing her calico dress in darkened corridors of the old hotel.

# CHAPTER FOURTEEN

# CALIFORNIA'S MONSTERS OF THE MOUNTAINS

From time to time strange stories of America's home-grown monsters, the Bigfoot, have cropped up in California. Residents of remote and desolate areas have reported giant apelike creatures who raid their chicken coops, carry off young calves, and knock over heavy construction equipment just for fun. Various Indian tribes of California have long-held legends that tell of the "ancient ones" or the "dark watchers," and some anthropologists have theorized about the possibility of a lost tribe of Indians who somehow maintain a Stone Age existence somewhere in the wilderness regions of California.

For nearly seventy years, mysterious deaths that occurred at a spot called Deadman's Hole in San Diego County, California, were attributed to one or more of these mysterious subhuman creatures.

The first victim of the monster of Deadman's Hole was an unidentified prospector whose mangled body was found by a stage driver in 1858. In 1888, a second victim was found in the same area, the circumstances of his death equally mysterious.

A resident of the area, William Blair, was found murdered at Deadman's Hole in 1922. Investigators reported that Blair's throat was discolored and bore the undeniable markings of massive fingers that had crushed out his life. It was also apparent that the victim had been dragged a great distance after he had been killed.

Whoever or *whatever* strangled William Blair had possessed incredible strength.

Within the year, an Indian girl named Belita was murdered by what appeared to have been the same powerful hands, and her crumpled body was discovered at the same spot at which the other victims had been located.

A few months after this death at Deadman's Hole, two area men, Edward Dean and Charles Cox, went into the canyon on a hunting trip. Alerted by the sounds of something heavy crashing through the brush before them, the hunters set out in pursuit of what they thought might be a large bear.

After several minutes of the chase, Cox turned to his companion and shouted, "That's no bear! It looks like a gorilla!"

Dean laughed at his friend's identification of their prey. He was about to chide Cox for drinking on the hunt when he caught a good glimpse of the creature for the first time. It certainly was not a bear. It walked upright with a strange, bobbing gait.

When Cox and Dean closed in on the beast, it turned toward them and began to rush them. For a dangerous moment, the men were frozen in fear, too stunned to react to the threat the monster posed.

"Its face was not unlike that of an Indian's," Dean said later to the authorities. "but its hands and feet were of monstrous size. They definitely were not humanlike."

At last Cox freed himself from the near fatal fascination the monster seemed to exert over them and shot the beast in its chest.

We will never know if the Monster of Deadman's Hole was a link to our Stone Age past, a remnant of a forgotten Indian tribe, an actual Bigfoot-type creature, or some giant recluse who had become demented and dangerous in his hermit's existence. Unfortunately, there are no records of an autopsy of the man-thing, nor is there any indication as to what may have become of the strange corpse.

Fortunately, however, for the residents in that area of San Diego County, there have been no mysterious reported slayings at Deadman's Hole since 1922.

The gold-seeking Spanish conquistadors were the first white men to listen incredulously as the California Indians told them of Bigfoot (*oh-mah*), the giant man-animal that disliked intruders in his forest domain.

"Do these creatures have any riches?" the Spanish officers wanted to know, theorizing that the *oh-mah* might be some strange guardian for the legendary Seven Cities of Gold.

The Indians laughed. "They do not even have fire. They wear no clothes. They live like animals, but are neither man nor animal."

The Spaniards soon lost interest in the *oh-mah*.

But the various Indian tribes have always retained their awareness of the *oh-mah*, the "dark watchers," and from time to time a white woodsman or homesteader caught a fleeting glimpse of the giant, apelike creature moving rapidly from tree to tree.

In 1833, at Lompock Ranch, California, soldiers were chopping through a layer of gravel when they unearthed the skeleton of a man they measured to be nearly twelve feet tall. The Indians all around the area became quite concerned about the skeleton, and it was obvious that they attributed special significance to the startling skeletal remains. A priest ordered the man-thing reburied secretly to quiet the stir that its discovery had created.

Whether the giant skeleton was that of a member of an unknown race of humans or that of a member of an unknown species of apelike creatures, for over a hundred years the *oh-mah* remained relegated to the realm of legend, emerging only to be blamed as possible suspects in such mysterious slayings as those at Deadman's Hole.

Then, in August 1958, a construction crew building a road through the rugged wilderness near Bluff Creek, Humboldt County, California, was startled one morning to discover gigantic,

humanlike footprints in the ground around their equipment. The sixteen-inch footprints revealed that their originator had a fifty- to sixty-inch stride. Overnight the term *Bigfoot* was coined to describe California's monsters of the mountains.

The nocturnal visitations continued for several days, and then the mysterious prowler decided to test his strength. The crew awoke one morning to find that someone—or *something*—had picked up an eight hundred-pound tire and wheel from an earth-moving machine and had carried it several yards across the equipment compound. The construction workers also discovered that a three hundred-pound steel drum of oil had been taken from their camp, carried up a rocky mountain slope, and heaved into a deep canyon.

It would have required the coordinated effort of several strong men to have lifted the loads carried by the prowling Bigfoot. Plaster casts were made of the giant footprints and, for once, the nation's press treated the subject matter seriously.

People began to step forward to be counted, telling of frightening encounters with hairy giants in California's forested mountain areas. Dozens of footprints were turned up in various sections of the state. Two doctors swore that they had almost run over a Bigfoot on Route 299 when the creature stepped in front of their speeding automobile. A woman and her two daughters reported sighting a similar apelike giant on a slope above the Hoopa Valley.

The Humboldt *Times* assigned reporter Betty Allen to do a series of interviews with the Yurok and Hoopa Indians. "So the white man has finally got around to the *oh-mah*," commented one Hoopa.

An elderly member of the Yurok clan of the Klamath tribe told the journalist that the Bigfoot had been quite numerous at one time, but they had been run out of the country by the gold hunters in 1849.

Not too long after the powerful prowler had struck the road-construction camp in August 1958, a motorist received the shock of his

life as he drove near Riverside in the San Bernardino Valley. According to twenty-four-year-old Charlie Wetzel, the frightening creature had "a round, scarecrowish head, like something out of Halloween," and it had incredibly long arms—one of which had reached inside and begun clawing at him before Wetzel sped off.

In February 1962, Robert Hatfield, a logger from Crescent City, California, was staying at the home of his friends Mr. and Mrs. Bud Jenkins of Fort Bragg. Late one night, Hatfield heard the dogs yelping in fear, and when he looked outside he saw what he thought was a giant bear peering over the fence at him.

After he had awakened Jenkins, Hatfield stepped outside to investigate, ran around a corner of the house, and collided with the creature. He was knocked sprawling to the ground, and when he looked up, he was staring into the face of a Bigfoot.

Hatfield began screaming to Jenkins to get back inside the house. "This thing is half-man, half-beast!"

The two men dashed into the house with the creature just a few steps behind Hatfield. As the Bigfoot howled and pushed against the door, the two men pressed against it with every ounce of their strength.

Suddenly the pressure on the door eased, and Jenkins ran to get his rifle. When he returned, their frightening visitor had disappeared, but he had left several huge footprints to corroborate their story. Measurements of a muddy handprint that Bigfoot had left on the side of the Jenkins house was eleven inches across at the palm.

For several years the residents of Tuolumne County, California, near the Yosemite National Forest, have reported Bigfoot activity in their area. Most of the witnesses there described the creature as an enormous, ten-foot-tall beast with a six- to eight-foot stride.

Late in December 1963, Sheriff's Deputy Albert Miller discovered several awesome tracks in freshly fallen snow near a garbage dump. "Those were no bear tracks," Miller insisted to newsmen.

"They measured sixteen inches by six inches wide, and there was six to eight feet between each print."

Another Bigfoot report came in January, when a pilot was flying low over Pinecrest and spotted a dark figure against the snow. He flew over the area again and reported that a "ten-foot man with ape like features" was standing in the snow.

The January 1964 sighting correlated in several details with a report filed a year earlier by a veteran bush pilot. He had been flying near Pinecrest on an aerial snow survey for the Pacific Gas and Electric Company when both he and a utility employee had seen a giant apelike creature standing in the snow. He banked the plane to photograph the Bigfoot, but the beast became alarmed and disappeared into a dense thicket.

In July, 1964, two young campers reported that a strange creature disturbed them while they were camping on Mount Tamalpais in Marin County, California.

Paul Conant, one of the campers, informed police officials that the thing was approximately five feet tall, had no tail, and had come near their camp.

"Its head was very close to its shoulders," he said, "and it was extremely muscular below the neck. I couldn't see any ears. There seemed to be another animal nearby, because we heard the two creatures chattering back and forth for around seven hours."

In the summer of 1967 James McClarin, a twenty-two-year-old zoology student at Humboldt State College, carved a monument to Bigfoot. The fourteen-foot redwood statue is located at the junction of highways 299 and 96 near Willow Creek, California, in the heart of the Six Rivers National Forest.

McClarin explained that he had carved the statue because he sincerely believed in the existence of Bigfoot. "Before I started to carve the statue, I spent four years investigating reports of Bigfoot. I met many people who have seen them. They're reputable citizens who

wouldn't lie or take part in a hoax. We've had at least forty reports on *oh-mahs* in the last few years. I've seen plaster casts and photographs of their footprints."

❖

After well over thirty years, the most convincing—and controversial—evidence for Bigfoot is Roger Patterson's movie film of a gigantic creature he photographed in the forest northwest of Eureka, California, on the afternoon of October 29, 1967. Patterson and Bob Gimlin were twenty miles beyond the end of a dirt road that had been slashed through the wilderness for logging trucks. The two men were moving through the dense underbrush when, without warning, their horses reared and tossed both riders to the ground.

Patterson rolled free of his horse and immediately set eyes on what had spooked his normally calm animal. Directly ahead of them was a gigantic, hairy animal walking upright like a human!

He scrambled for his 16mm movie camera. After years of searching, Patterson was focusing on a female Bigfoot. He hand-held his camera, dashing through the brush toward the woodswoman, trying to keep focus on her. The female Bigfoot was walking away; then, suddenly, she stopped and looked back toward Patterson and Gimlin.

The two excited monster-hunters had their film carefully developed and had additional prints made. After they had securely placed the original in a fireproof vault, they next screened the film for the Documentary Film Department at Universal Pictures. Patterson and Gimlin challenged the special-effects technicians to duplicate the film.

"Impossible!" the technicians replied. "Give us a few million, and we might try it. First, we'd have to create a new set of artificial muscles, then train an actor to walk like that thing, and then put him into a gorilla-skin."

Excited by this professional response, Patterson and Gimlin invited various scientists to view the film. The academic community was simply not interested then and remains aloof to the mystery of Bigfoot to this day.

✦

Academic acceptance of the enigma of Bigfoot means little to those men and women who have experienced firsthand encounters with the creature. Harold B. Nelson, a retired grocer from suburban Los Angeles, said that he was so terrified that he could "hardly blink his eyes," and it really doesn't matter to him if every college professor in the world doubts his story. He knows that it happened.

Nelson had been driving for several hours on a hot afternoon in September 1968 when he pulled his pickup camper off the road to take a little rest and to have a small snack. He had barely stepped out of the cab to stretch his legs when he found himself staring directly into the face of a huge Bigfoot.

"I was frozen with terror," he said. "No one can imagine the sudden shock during an experience like that. It had an apelike face, but I know it was definitely not a gorilla. The head was slightly pointed, sloping downward as we've seen in depictions of cavemen. The entire body was covered with a reddish-brown hair, and it was standing erect on two feet, like a man. There were a few patches of white hair along the fringes of his shoulders. And that sonofagun was huge. He must have weighed six or seven hundred pounds. And when he straightened up, he must have stood over seven feet tall. He was real big!"

Nelson now supposes that he must also have surprised the Bigfoot. "It jumped back when I shined my flashlight in its face, and it made a weird noise—like a cross between a deep gargle and a scream. I sobbed with absolute relief when the beast turned away and shuffled off into the darkness."

Bigfoot sightings have not abated, and the mystery monster of the California mountains remains as elusive as ever. In November 1989, a man who wishes to be known only as Dwight had an encounter with a Bigfoot while he was hiking somewhere in the Bluff Creek area.

"I was situated in a position where I could see the creature coming from a considerable distance off," Dwight began. "At first, I supposed that I was seeing a bear, and I became immediately cautious. I had a .22 rifle with me, but that would have been useless against an angry bear.

"Then I saw an honest-to-goodness kind of ape man coming toward my hiding place. I had heard about Bigfoot for years, but because I spend as much time as possible in the wilderness and I had never seen one, I had concluded that the stories must be hoaxes or overly imaginative interpretations of known wildlife.

"As this huge creature kept coming toward me, I started to become very nervous," Dwight continued. "It was easily six and a half feet tall, and it had to weigh well over four hundred pounds. I played a lot of football in high school and college, and I, myself, am no lightweight; but I had no interest in arm-wrestling this huge dude.

"I'm kind of ashamed to admit it, but when it kept coming closer, I got really scared, and I completely lost it. I stood up, shouted, and fired a couple of rounds in the air."

Dwight stated that the Bigfoot froze in its tracks, did a double take when it saw the hiker with the rifle, and took off running in the opposite direction.

"Dear God, I was so relieved that the thing was actually scared witless by me," Dwight admitted. "I don't know what I would have done if it had charged me. I am really glad that I frightened it off."

Dwight conceded that many people to whom he has told his story have chided him for permitting the scientific find of the century to get away from him. Several have wondered why he didn't shoot the Bigfoot and turn its body over to scientists for a complete analysis.

"People have told me that I could have solved the mystery of Bigfoot once and for all," Dwight said. "Well, I figure, if the mystery is supposed to be solved, it will happen one day without killing one of the things. And if someone should happen to kill one and turn its body over to science, I personally am very glad that I was not that person.

"To be honest," Dwight explained, "the thing looked too human to me. I couldn't have shot it—unless maybe it had attacked me.

"The more that I have thought about it, I think that Bigfoot is probably a lower form of human being. Maybe they're really some kind of primitive species. I honestly believe that it would be murder to kill one."

# CHAPTER FIFTEEN

# THE DEADLY TREASURES
# OF TIBURÓN

In 1893, an English naval lieutenant named Robinson and three friends arrived in a tiny village of what has since become Sonora state, a province of Mexico located next to the Baja California peninsula. From their position on the coast, they could look across the choppy blue waters of the Gulf of California at the long and level stretch of land known as the Isla Tiburón.

Of the four, Lieutenant Robinson was the only one who had ever been in the area before; it was he who had talked the others into coming. But Robinson did not have to do very much more than mention nineteen million minted gold pesos to his friends, and they were hauling him down to the Liverpool docks and onto a ship bound for Mexico. Robinson had passed through Baja California once before on Her Majesty's business, but this second trip was strictly a private affair; and the English adventurers hoped that it would also be a lucrative one.

The lieutenant had learned from reliable and independent sources that a vast store of minted gold coins had been buried on the beaches of the island by Mexican nobility, eager to save what they could of the fortunes that were being liquidated out from under them during the Mexican Revolution. The reports had hardened him into one of the most determined treasure-seekers ever to cross the ocean.

Thus it was disappointing that they could find no one in the Mexican village who would ferry them the short distance out to the island that held the fabulous treasure.

"It is no good to go there," one villager told them in broken English. "My friends, nothing but death awaits you there."

Robinson had heard weird stories about the Seri Indian tribe that inhabited the island, but he had not put much stock in the blood-thirsty tales. The villagers, however, were unanimous in refusing to take the group across to the island. The English treasure-hunters tried everyone in the village capable of holding a paddle before they became convinced that no one would ferry them across.

Indians or no Indians, Robinson and his friends were determined to get across the channel and have a chance at the nineteen million coins. Robinson's desire for the treasure was fanned by its proximity and by the many tales with which he was familiar. Robinson had heard of the Italian priest who had returned from Tiburón with nearly forty thousand English pounds worth of pearls and gold he had received in trade from the Seri. There was also the tale of the two prospectors, who, in 1879, had spent a week on the island panning placer gold out of the sand on the beach. Although the Seri had run them off, their net profit for a week's worth of sifting the sand six feet under the beach level was eight thousand dollars worth of placer gold.

Robinson and crew ended up buying two dugouts from a villager, who was even reluctant to sell them the boats, and they managed to make it across the treacherous water without benefit of a guide.

The first night Robinson and his friends spent on the beaches of the island was virtually uneventful. The only anxious moments occurred when an ancient-looking crone wandered near their fire and stood gawking at them for a few seconds before disappearing into the night. A bit later, several of her male counterparts appeared around the fire. The old men seemed friendly enough, and the treasure-hunters exchanged gifts of greeting with them.

After the elderly Indians had left them, the Englishmen wondered aloud why the people on the mainland had thought them hostile.

The following day, Robinson and his party staked out the area in which they had decided to dig, and they were even successful in hiring a few of the younger Indians to help to do some spadework.

But digging had barely got underway when a screaming horde of Seri with hideously painted faces began running at the Englishmen, waving spears and muskets. Robinson and his friends, who had been napping pleasantly, were now staring into faces more terrifying than any they had seen in their most grotesque nightmares.

One of the men never made it to his feet before he was pinioned to the beach by several spears. Robinson and the other two men ran for the canoes.

The naval lieutenant was not as swift as the Seri, however, and his retreating friends saw what must be rated as one of the most grisly sights in the annals of treasure-hunting, as Robinson's body was mashed to a pulp by a cascade of stones wielded by the Indians.

❖

Tiburón, located off the coast of Baja California, about four hundred miles south of San Diego, is a twenty-by-thirty-mile stretch of fiercely rough scrub country. The murder of Lieutenant Robinson and his friends would not be the last time that men seeking the fabled wealth of Tiburón would meet death at the hands of the island's fierce inhabitants.

Even before the white man set foot on North America, the Seri Indians were an anachronism when compared with their sophisticated Aztec neighbors. Labeled the most primitive extant tribe in the Western Hemisphere, the Seri have meant trouble to three eras of government in Mexico, and only the severe depletion of their numbers in recent times has made their savagery a relatively minor concern today.

In one sense, it is an accident of nature that the tribe's homeland contains some of the wealthiest ground in the world. A few successful prospectors have sifted placer gold out of the sand on the beach and have lived to tell about it. There is every indication that

the natural deposits of gold on the island are exceedingly rich.

But in another sense, the wealth of the island is not an accident at all. In succession, the Aztec, Spanish, and Mexican nobility were pushed out of Mexico, and the wealth that they had stored was never completely captured by the incoming conquerors. In numerous instances, some of those treasure troves ended up on Tiburón—for good reason. The reputation of the Seri as a bloodthirsty lot who feasted on human flesh to absorb the strength of their victims was well known, even in Aztec times. The retreating regimes, whether Aztec hierarchy or Spanish lords, were not about to leave their booty where a farmer might uncover it with his plow. Rather, they elected to risk hiding their treasure on a deserted beach that was protected by a horde of cannibalistic natives. Later, they could return to the island, go directly to the exact spot, and retrieve the loot—hopefully without disturbing the Seri. In the meantime, the cache would be safe from any treasure-hunter, whose search would probably take days or weeks—and whose presence would certainly be discovered by the Seri in that amount of time.

It is doubtful that the Seri Indians were ever informed that they served as the guardians for the treasure troves of so many generations, and it is even more doubtful that they would have appreciated their unique position if they had. The Seri society appears to have been built on a hatred of everything that was not Seri, excluding human flesh for their cooking pots. The history of the tall, powerfully built tribe's relations with the ruling powers of Mexico is a record of an extremely tenacious people, stubbornly holding to their traditional homeland with such strength that army after army could not dislodge them.

The seemingly ridiculous situation of the savages of Tiburón defeating well-armed soldiers of a technologically advanced world went on for generations until an uneasy truce was arranged between the Seri and the Mexican government. A good portion of the tribe even moved to the mainland, where it was more comfortable to live.

Tragically, the Seri continued in their primitive ways and, as it

turned out, these customs were not compatible with those of the sur-rounding Mexican people. For instance, while the Seri deemed horse rustling a perfectly honorable pursuit, the Mexicans took a dim view of such a practice. When a local nobleman had a Seri executed for such thievery, the entire tribe rose up in mass revolt, terrorizing entire villages, killing women and children indiscriminately. This proved too much for the Mexicans to bear, and in a war of vengeance, heavily armed troops wiped out practically every Seri on the mainland.

During those times when the Seri remained on their island, pro-tected against the outside world by the rough, cactus-covered country that they knew best, they were practically undefeatable. But when they manned their war canoes to venture to the main-land, they became easy prey for the techniques of a much more deadly method of warfare. In a decade of conflict, a powerful tribe of 35,000 was reduced to just 350 members, who headed back at last to the safety of Tiburón.

Even in such limited numbers it soon became apparent that the Seri were not people to be ignored.

Two Americans went to the island in 1895, but only one of them returned. George Porter, a sea captain, and a sailor named Johnson tried a new approach. They came in on the back side of Tiburón, traversing dangerous shoals to do so, but thereby avoiding the Seri.

Porter and Johnson searched the oyster shoals for pearls, the beaches for gold—and, according to Johnson, who escaped, they found a little of each. But the Seri put a stop to their treasure hunt and killed and dismembered Porter in the process.

In 1904, two prospectors searching for pitchblende wandered on the island. It is not known whether or not they made a strike, because nothing more was heard or seen of them except for two skulls fastened to a piece of wood with a camera strap.

The death of the prospectors brought on another expedition against the Seri. Once again, even though severely outnumbered, the tribe of Tiburón survived the onslaught.

With such fierce guardians, it is no wonder that so little of the wealth of the island has been carried off.

# CHAPTER SIXTEEN

# PADRE ISLAND—PARADISE FOR TREASURE-HUNTERS

Sandy, sunny, desolate Padre Island, which lies a scant two miles off the coast of Texas, is a veritable paradise for every type of treasure-hunter. Due to its unusual shape and unique location, this fabulous sandbar in the Gulf of Mexico receives tons of wreckage each year.

Padre Island has become a natural safety deposit box for the sea. Bizarre hulls of wrecked shrimp boats, rotting timbers of ancient, ill-fated ships, and the flotsam and jetsam of the sea find a final resting place on the sandy, barren beaches—along with unfound booty that professional treasure-hunters have estimated at three billion dollars in sunken, buried, or hidden loot.

Formed at the mouth of the Rio Grande near Port Isabel, the treasure-filled strip of sand extends northeastward along the Texas coast for 132 miles and ends near Port Arkansas. A strange and mysterious area by any standard, Padre Island is no more than three miles wide at its broadest point. The raging waves of countless storms have slimmed the island down to a bare quarter-of-a-mile width at other points.

Once the center of a bustling cattle kingdom, the island is now barren and unused. The lengthy strip of sand is seldom utilized for anything more than fishing, sunbathing, and treasure-hunting.

Spanish pieces of eight and chests crammed with rare coins have

often been washed onto the beaches of Padre Island. In 1933, a woman who was searching for unique pieces of driftwood spied a box in the sand. It contained a handful of coins, jewels, and valuable artifacts.

In 1962, W. F. Jackson, Vernon Jackson, and Wayne Jackson of Edcouch, Texas, were fishing from the island. Spotting a glint of metal in the sand, they scooped up a handful of blackened, corroded coins. Cleaned and polished, the coins revealed Spanish mint dates of 1530 to 1560 and proved to be solid silver.

Old-timers on Padre Island tell the story of a recent vacationer whose afternoon beach stroll was interrupted by his find of a half-buried chest in the sandy loam. The lucky vacationer left the island with more than ten thousand dollars in coins that had been minted during the reign of Charles I and Joanna of Spain in the early sixteenth century.

Another fortunate vacationer was a high school teacher from New York City, a scuba enthusiast. The teacher and his wife had spent the entire summer diving in the clear waters around the island. Although they protested that they were not serious treasure-seekers, by summer's end they had collected a canvas bag brimming with dozens of old bottles, Spanish specie, rare artifacts, and valuable antiques.

Whenever a storm pummels the island, things are stirred up, and experienced treasure-hunters rush to the beach. When Hurricane Carla struck Padre Island on September 11, 1961, the vicious winds of the storm blew away tons of sand to reveal the long-lost city of Southmost. In 1875, a gigantic hurricane had blown the town into oblivion, covering it with tons of sand. The town, located on the American or landward side, was once an important port for Southwest shipping and had been a leading trade center during the Civil War.

Armed with metal detectors, vacationing treasure-hunters can find the Padre beaches extremely profitable. An electronic signal may indicate the presence of a rusting ship's nail—or a bar of silver. Seekers of lost loot have found Spanish coins, boxes of jewels, Civil War relics, Indian artifacts, and rare pre-Columbian art objects.

How did such booty come to Padre Island?

After the discovery of the New World, the Spaniards' quest for gold soon led to Mexico. After their first battle with the Aztec nation, the conquistadors were astonished to find that many of the slaughtered Indians wore jewelry cast of pure gold.

When word of the "golden warriors" reached the homeland, the stampede of fortune-hunters reached frantic proportions. In an effort to placate the foreign devils' insatiable appetite for the shiny metal, the great Aztec chieftain Montezuma offered them huge plates of solid gold. The bountiful attempt at appeasement merely sharpened the Spaniards' hunger for more loot and treasure.

The invaders seized the legendary treasure of the Aztecs, stripping temples, melting jewelry, and using native slave labor to work the mines. The treasure of Montezuma was shipped to Spain on three bulging caravels. These small ships were to be escorted to Cádiz from Cape St. Vincent by an armada of Spanish warships.

While rounding the Azores, however, a lookout shouted "Pirates!" Eventually all three of the treasure ships were seized by the crafty Dieppe buccaneer Jean Fleury.

Undaunted, the Spanish soldiers sought more gold in the seemingly inexhaustible mystery cities of the New World. When Pizarro conquered the Inca empire, he imprisoned Atahualpa, its chief, in an 18-by-23-foot cell. When the Incas sought to ransom their leader, Pizarro set the terms that they must bring him a volume of gold equal to the size of Atahualpa's cell.

Dutifully, Inca temples were stripped, items of personal jewelry were melted down, and enough gold was at last assembled to satisfy the gold-fixated Pizarro. Treacherously, the Spaniards then condemned the Inca chief to be burned.

With so many tons of gold flowing into the imperial coffers, Spain needed better sea transportation. They set about constructing a fleet of huge galleons—big-bellied vessels with enormous sails for fast speed and high sides to resist boarding by pirates.

In 1503, the Spanish royal family formed the Casa de Contratación, headquartered in Seville, to control the imperial "golden fleet." The Casa, with bureaucratic thoroughness, orga-

nized every detail of siphoning off the riches of the New World.

The Casa decreed a single convoy each year. Sailing from Cádiz in the first fortnight in May, the departing ships carried merchandise and supplies to the fledgling settlements in the Americas. They returned loaded with gold and silver.

Although the great convoys lessened the possibility of losing vessels to preying pirates, the logistics of coordinating the movements of such an armada created other problems. As the convoy approached the New World, it was necessary that it split up in order to service various ports. Months later, the need to rendezvous at a selected site meant that the galleons often had to sail in bad weather so that they would not miss the protection of the convoy of the return journey.

The losses were terrible. In the first six years covered by the Casa's records, 159 ships set forth for the New World and only 101 returned. In the first twelve years of transporting gold, more than 45 percent of the Spanish fleet was wrecked, lost, or destroyed. Treacherous currents and the slashing winds of hurricanes drove many ships onto sharp reefs and then smashed them to splinters.

One of the most horrendous disasters was the loss of fifteen treasure-filled galleons off Vera Cruz, Mexico. Battered by a raging tempest, the fleet sank to the harbor bottom.

From the time the first Spanish ship arrived in Mexico, the Spaniards had been aware of Padre Island. It began to be used as a rendezvous for ships departing from various ports, and several ships had run aground in the shallow waters around the island.

In 1553, a fleet of sixteen galleons left Vera Cruz for the annual rendezvous. The lashing winds of a hurricane trapped the fleet and drove the wooden ships onto hidden reefs. Thirteen of the ships sank around Padre Island. Casa records, always meticulously maintained, indicate that three ships went to a watery grave near latitude 26½ degrees north, in the general vicinity of Texas' Baffin Bay.

Three hundred surviving seamen made it to shore, reported the Casa, but nearly all of them were seized and eaten by the cannibal tribe of Karankawa Indians. A lone survivor made it back to Vera Cruz.

Cargo in the holds of the ill-fated vessels included four million dollars in gold and silver. Rotting hulls of once proud Spanish galleons rest on the ocean floor from Port Isabel up to Port Arkansas.

Diving for these unclaimed millions in treasure could mean sudden wealth for the lucky scuba enthusiast. Here is a brief record of a few treasure-laden ships that sank off Padre Island:

An unidentified Spanish galleon went down in 1811. This mystery ship was known to be carrying fifty thousand dollars in gold, and reports indicate that the ship sank quickly after hitting a reef.

The *Little Fleta* sank off the coast, near La Balsa, Texas, in 1874, with thirty thousand dollars in its ship's safe.

Hidden somewhere under the waves off Brazos, Texas, is the *S. J. Lee*, which went down during the great storm of 1875 and rests in a scant eighteen feet of water. The wreck contained $150,000 in gold and silver, and a passenger is said to have carried a small chest of jewels aboard the ship.

The *Texas Ranger* also sank near the Brazos area in 1875. It carried a reported two hundred thousand dollars on board. Another victim of the storm of 1875 was the *Ida Lewis*. She found a wet grave near Brazos and took twenty thousand dollars with her to the deep.

The *Clara Woodhouse*, carrying eighty thousand dollars and a possible cargo of silver bars, also rests on the bottom of the Gulf of Mexico near Brazos, Texas, where she sank sometime in the late 1870s.

The *Carrie Thomas* made her final voyage in 1880 with $140,000 on board. She went down below Rio Grande City, Texas, in the then-navigable Rio Grande.

In 1882 the *Lea* sank near the *Carrie Thomas* to a final resting place in the muddy silt. The ship carried a hundred thousand dollars on board.

In 1914 the *E. P. Wright*, a schooner, was outward bound past the Brazos Santiago Pass when she went down with a hundred thousand dollars aboard in gold and silver. The cargo also consisted of a large amount of guns and ammunition.

In 1931 the *Columbia* floundered near the Brazos Santiago Pass and sank with eight hundred thousand dollars locked in her hold.

The waters outside the Brazos Santiago Pass claimed many a merchantman during World War II. German U-boats hid just outside the pass and torpedoed an untold number of merchant ships.

## THE STRANGE TREASURE OF JOHN SINGER

John Singer, a brother of the man who manufactured the sewing machine of the same name, was an individualist who shaped his own destiny. In 1847, during a treacherous storm, Singer was shipwrecked on Padre Island.

While other survivors loudly cursed their bad luck, Singer peered reflectively through the ferocious winds. "This would be a perfect place for a cattle ranch," he announced to his astonished fellows.

Later, Singer settled near Lost City, which is about twenty-three miles north of Brazos Santiago Pass, and established a large cattle ranch. For several years the hard-driving Yankee poured money and time into his ranch. His efforts paid off—but in a way never dreamed of by the rancher.

One afternoon while he was excavating for the foundation of a house, Singer's spade struck a metallic object. Curious, he managed to unearth the obstacle and he soon found himself staring in wonder at a metal sea chest.

Recalling many an old-timer's stories of buried pirate treasure, Singer smashed the locks on the chest. Gleaming doubloons, shiny silver coins, and glittering jewels glistened in the sunlight. Realizing that he had uncovered a fortune, the rancher carried the chest home.

That evening, in the soft glow of candlelight, he catalogued the contents of the sea chest. The bonanza was easily worth ninety thousand dollars in the hard money days of pre-Civil War America. Today, the fabulous chest of riches would be worth from five hundred thousand dollars to eight hundred thousand dollars.

As the years passed, John Singer's cattle ranch prospered and added its profits to his wealth. Then the Civil War pitted brother against brother, and Padre Island became of strategic importance to both Union and Confederate governments. Whoever controlled

Padre Island ultimately dominated Southwestern shipping. Soon patrols of both Confederate and Union troops were tramping over the sand dunes, fighting minor skirmishes—and keeping a sharp eye cocked for treasure.

At last, John Singer decided to abandon his ranch until after the war and to move his family to the Texas mainland. Assuming that he would never be able to slip the treasure or their family heirlooms past the military patrols, Singer decided his best course was to bury everything and come back to recover it after the hostilities were ended.

He deposited the pirate booty, his family heirlooms, and an unknown amount of ranching profits in a cast-iron tub. He left the ranchhouse alone and went off to bury the treasure. He recorded the location on a map. All his family knew was that several small chests were buried in locations along the mahogany driftwood fenceposts of the ranch. The giant tub was interred midway between two oak trees.

His personal fortune safely secured beneath the sands of Padre Island, Singer loaded his family into a boat. By carefully paddling past night patrols, they managed to make their way to Port Isabel.

After the war, John Singer returned to Padre Island to reclaim his vast treasure. He was appalled to discover that several raging storms had completely destroyed Lost City.

Hurrying to his ranch, Singer found the fenceposts still standing, and he recovered several of his small chests of gold. The giant tub of booty was a different matter.

Tracing his route by map, Singer could no longer find any sign of the two oak trees. His carefully drawn map was worthless.

John Singer continued his luckless search until his death. His son took up the search for the lost family treasure until he, too, died in 1945. The Singer treasure has never been recovered.

Somewhere beneath the shifting sands of Padre Island is a modern-day fortune in gold and jewels. The changing sands may one day reveal the giant tub to the view of some passing beachcomber or weekend treasure-seeker, and the fortunate finder will be rich beyond his dreams.

# CHAPTER SEVENTEEN

# UNFOUND TREASURE TROVES IN THE LONE STAR STATE

Sunken galleons filled with precious specie. Gold doubloons washed ashore on a sunny beach. Legendary lost mines said to be guarded by the ghosts of sun-bleached skeletons. Buried bandit booty and graves filled with bags of coins and precious jewels.

These and other equally alluring legends of bountiful Texas treasure troves make the Lone Star state one of the world's most promising regions for the discovery of unclaimed caches of gold and precious booty. Successively under four flags, its history brimming with revolutions, wars, Indian raids, and foreign armies, Texas is rich in the folkfore of lost loot. And to the delight of the enthusiastic treasure-hunter, a good many of these legends are true and well-documented.

The general locations of the famous unfound Texas treasures described in this chapter are often known, but the ravages of time and the erosion of nature may have dramatically altered the landscape. Landmarks left by the men who buried the treasure are often obliterated. The quick-growing back-country brush will hide a clue, and the shifting sands of the dust-dry country can change the terrain of the countryside.

# A Cannon Barrel Filled with Gold in the Neches River

Scuba enthusiasts who are not put off by the mud and silt of the Neches River will be interested in the strange claim of a sunken cannon that contains a Mexican army payroll.

In 1836, with political emotions at a boiling point, border skirmishes were regular occurrences. One afternoon, a band of fight-hungry Texans came upon a group of Mexicans along the Neches River, near the Boone's Ferry crossing. During the ensuing gun battle, the Texans were surprised to see the Mexicans pull a large artillery cannon to the crest of a hill and roll it over a cliff into the muddy depths of the river.

After the defeat of the Mexicans, the Texans were told by their prisoners that the cannon had been consigned to a watery grave to prevent its use against Mexico. There was no reason to discount this.

Several years after the incident and after the shooting war between Mexico and the Texans had subsided, a young Mexican arrived at Boone's Ferry and set about hiring several residents of the area to aid him in a search for the cannon. According to the story told by old-timers, the young man's father had been with the Mexicans in the Boone's Ferry battle. The detachment had been transporting a payroll of gold, and when the commander had perceived that defeat at the hands of the Texans was imminent, he had ordered the young Mexican's father to stuff sixty thousand dollars in gold coins into the barrel of the cannon and roll it into the river.

The Mexican gave up his search after several months, and he had barely spurred his horse toward the south before Texas organized several frantic expeditions to recover the cannon. One man devoted many years of his life in a vain attempt to locate the elusive artillery piece, but he, too, eventually surrendered to time.

One reason that the cannon has never been discovered may be that the river is filled with soft mud along the stretch where it was jettisoned. The cannon may now be many feet below the river bed. The changing course of the river may also have prevented the cannon's recovery.

## SEVEN BURROS LADEN WITH
## LOOT BURIED ON A BRAZOS BLUFF

Another Texas treasure that has defied all efforts for recovery lies buried somewhere up the east fork of the Brazos River. Clues to the exact location of the treasure do not exist, although the final breath of a dying prospector reported the general location.

In the early days of the Texas Republic, a band of ore-laden prospectors were returning down the Brazos River. They had been away from civilization for several months, chipping vast quantities of silver and gold from the barren terrain. They would soon be home, and each man recited his own thoughts of how he would celebrate.

Distracted by their visions of wine and women, the prospectors neglected to scout the land ahead. As war whoops filled the early morning air, the miners discovered too late that their party was surrounded by Indians.

Fleeing to a nearby bluff, the men blasted away at wave after wave of the attacking war party. During a lull in the battle, the prospectors formed a circle to discuss their options.

The miners decided that they would never be able to escape the war party with the ore they had collected. They deemed their best chance lay in burying the booty there and slipping out during the night. Seven burros were stripped of their heavy cargo, and the gold and silver were lowered into a hastily excavated hole. Once this task was completed, the prospectors dusted the area to eliminate any signs of digging.

As a full moon rose in the eastern sky, the miners shook hands and declared that it was every man for himself from here on out. As the men slipped off the bluff and into the night, the Indians were waiting for them. Knives glinted in the moonlight, and all but one miner fell under the hostile blades.

Wounded, more dead than alive, the lone survivor stumbled into a mission down river several days later. "Seven burros ... gold and silver ... buried on a bluff," he gasped to a priest, then joined his comrades in death.

103

Few people have sought the elusive treasure of the seven burros. Clues to the location are scarce. Yet if the last words of a dying prospector can be believed, a fortune in gold and silver rests only scant feet under the soil.

## THE ROCK PENS TREASURE

Dan Dunham, gunfighter, bandit, adventurer, took what he wanted with the assistance of a brace of cocked sixguns. After a plundering expedition into Old Mexico, Dunham and his gang were attacked by hostile Indians. Badly wounded, the gunfighter escaped and left six million dollars in gold and silver buried beneath the Texas soil.

Before he died in Austin on April 17, 1873, Dunham left precise instructions for the recovery of his treasure:

"About six or seven miles below the Loredo Crossing on the south side of the Nueces River, near the hills, there is or was a tree in the prairie. Due west from that tree, at the foot of the hills, at the mouth of a ravine, there is a large rock. Under the rock there is (or was) a small spring of water coming from under the rock. Due east from that rock is a rock pen, or rocks laid around like a pen, and due east a few yards there is another rock pen. In that rock pen are the spoils of 31 mule loads."

No one has ever recovered the Rock Pens treasure, for the terrain and the landscape around the region do not coincide with the directions left by Dan Dunham. Many treasure seekers believe that the old gunfighter may have erred in his knowledge of the region.

## SUBLETT'S MINE

One of the most famous legendary figures of the Old Southwest, cantankerous Ben Sublett, used to wander into El Paso with brimming bagfuls of gold nuggets. Altogether, it is estimated that the secretive prospector took more than two hundred thousand dollars out of his still-unfound mine in the Guadalupe Mountains, and millions more are said to remain for the lucky treasure-hunter.

Ross Sublett, the prospector's son, visited the mine as a young man and later reported his recollection of seeing "nuggets just lying around on the ground." Although the younger Sublett knew that the location of the mine was somewhere between El Paso and Odessa, he failed to find the proper piece of Texas landscape after his father's death. The nuggets are still waiting there for someone to retrieve.

## STEINHEIMER'S BURIED MILLIONS

A German-born adventurer, who sailed with pirates, rode with bandits, and worked the slave trade, Karl Steinheimer buried a vast amount of gold dust and nuggets in Texas. Steinheimer himself estimated the treasure at more than five hundred thousand dollars. Today it would probably be worth fifteen times that sum.

According to Steinheimer's deathbed letter to his fiancée, the treasure lies north of Austin, "where three streams intersect and flow into one." This location is quite likely the junction of the Salado, Lampassas, and Little rivers.

The only other clue was Steinheimer's statement that he drove a copper spike into an oak tree to mark the treasure site shortly before his expedition was overrun by raiding Indians.

## THE LEGENDARY LOST SAN SABA MINES

The story of the lost San Saba mines, which may be worth as much as two hundred million dollars, began in the 1750s, when early Spaniards constructed a mission between the Llano and Colorado rivers. The mission served both as a center for Christianity and as a secret base for gold and silver safaris into the surrounding area.

Within a few miles of the mission, gold-seeking Spanish soldiers had discovered numerous mines and had profitably worked several of them. The soft, rich ore was smelted and poured into ingots, shipped to the mission, then sent on to Mexico and eventually across the sea to Spain.

Although the mines remained at levels of high productivity, it was the lack of water, coupled with marauding bands of bandits and Indians, that caused the Spaniards to seal the mines. Old church records in Monclova, Mexico, reveal the initial discovery of the mines by Don Bernardo de Miranda, a lieutenant general in the Spanish province of Texas. Overwhelmed by the potential riches he had assessed, Don Bernardo succumbed to a most generous impulse when he wrote that the mine was so rich that he would give every settler in the province a full claim.

The Spaniards abandoned the mines in 1758 when two thousand Comanche warriors overran their mission base. Don Bernardo said that the legendary bonanza mines were on the Cerro del Almagre—loosely translated, the Red Hill.

A geologist, who spent a great deal of effort searching for the mines, stated that he believed that the San Saba treasure trove would be found near Red Hill, a community of three hundred about seven miles south of Bend. Five dark-red boulders covered the entrance to the mines, and they contrasted sharply with the slate-gray dolomite limestone.

T. S. Lemons, Sr., purchased thirty-three hundred acres, including Red Hill, in 1944, and he once said that he had always been curious about the five red boulders on his land.

One afternoon in August 1964 his son, T. S., Jr., forty, was fishing in the Colorado River near the Red Hill. Noticing the shiny glint of a rock in the river, he chipped off a sample and put it in his pocket. Months later, he asked Arville Cummins to assay the rock.

Cummins had studied geology and had worked with rock samples all his adult life. He decreed that there was gold in T. S., Jr.'s sample. It wasn't "really big," he noted, but a commercial firm officially assayed it at $29.50 a ton, enough for a mining company to make money on a dig.

T. S., Jr., and Cummins explored the region around the river in the hope of discovering the source of the ore. Less than a mile from Red Hill, a short distance from Dead Man's Canyon, they discovered a tree with some old, nearly indecipherable markings carved into the bark. Clearly visible was a semicircle carved directly above

a V. Beneath the V was a straight horizontal line. As many a sea-soned treasure-hunter knows, a half moon is the ancient universal map symbol for treasure.

The Texans secured a metal detector, and the machine indicated a large metallic deposit under the tree. They dug to a depth of five feet, but abandoned the hole when evidence of an old smelter was found about a mile from Red Hill. There was also the discovery of three holes that had been drilled into the limestone wall of a ravine of Red Hill.

Eventually, the treasure-hunters came to the five red boulders. Four were blasted, and the fifth was preserved as a memento by the elder Lemons. The Texans set about digging on the spot where the boulders had rested.

They were disillusioned when their first ore sample assayed out at only $3.15 a ton in gold. At the depth of around twenty feet, the value of the samples soared to $29.90, the same as the ore found in the river.

Cummins and the younger Lemons stopped at this point to form a corporation with two other men. The land was leased by the elder Lemons, who would receive royalties in the event of a suc-cessful mining operation. The new partners were Arville Cummins' father Aaron, a retired grocer, and R. R. McCoy, a Lampasa, Texas, contractor. Two months later, a road had been carved down the rocky hill to the site of the proposed mine.

Blasting and sampling began anew. Two weeks later, ore was dis-covered that assayed at $3.75 a ton. Then, at a depth of thirty-five feet, ore was brought up that Cummins tested at $350 a ton!

When none of his partners could believe Cummins' assessment of the richness of the sample, they insisted that the ore be sent to a commercial assaying firm for a second opinion. They were all astonished when the deeper ore assayed at $467.50 a ton. In addi-tion, the sample also contained $150 to $190 a ton of molybdenum, a mineral used to strengthen steel.

But was the lucky find made by the Texas treasure-hunters truly the legendary San Saba mines? A lot of students of lost mines think not.

"I think the old San Saba, the true San Saba is still out there somewhere," is the way one seasoned treasure-hunter stated his opinion.

"The old church records say that the Spaniards placed a lot of ingots in the mines before they sealed them. I haven't heard of any ingots being found at Red Hill. As far as I am concerned, there's still two hundred million in Spanish gold waiting for me or for someone somewhere around Bend, Texas!"

# CHAPTER EIGHTEEN

# EARL DORR'S LOST RIVER OF GOLD IN THE DESERT

Near Barstow, California, there is a reported but untapped underground river of gold. Flowing through an intricate network of subterranean caves, this bonanza stream has twice been discovered—then lost again.

The man who is said to have found this nugget-filled stream of untapped riches was Earl Dorr, a man who had always been enchanted by the lure of desert gold. Although frustration, futility, and failure were his constant companions, Earl kept on checking out old Indian legends of Spanish gold mines.

Then, one evening in the 1920s, Earl Dorr's luck changed, and his life was never the same again. He had been prospecting in a treacherous strip of mountains east of Barstow, and in order to escape the searing heat of the desert he had camped in the cool mouth of a cave.

After sundown, a bright moon cast a silver glow across the eerie landscape as Dorr ate his usual dinner of hardtack bread and beans.

Despite a long day of futile explorations, Dorr's reckless spirit prompted him to investigate the interior of the cave. A seasoned desert prospector, he was well aware that a cave can be a welcome refuge from the blistering heat—or a deadly den of angry rattlers. A weapon was a necessity, and Dorr belted a holstered revolver

around his waist. Then, slinging a lengthy coil of rope over his shoulder, he adjusted his carbide miner's lamp and began to follow the cave tunnel into the mountain.

The sandy, powder-dry floor of the outer tunnel quickly turned into a wet, slippery passageway. The floor of the cave was filled with perilous, slime-walled black pits that slanted downward like treacherous, open traps. As he approached the craters, Dorr methodically lowered himself into each one and explored their interiors. Most ended in a stifling, stench-filled, empty bottom.

There were myriad passageways leading off from the main tunnel of the cave, and Dorr investigated each branch. After several hours, the persistent prospector discovered a tunnel leading downward from the main passageway. His explorations were taking him deeper and deeper into the heart of the cave.

The passageway ended suddenly in an immense wall of stone. Dorr's spirits plummeted until the flickering flame of his carbide lamp caught the shadow of a circular, knee-high opening in the wall. This tunnel also led downward, and the prospector's descent was a precarious step-by-step process.

The small tunnel opened into an immense, tomblike room.

Giant stalactites hung from the ceiling. Dorr's fascination with the eerie environment was interrupted by the bubbling sound of running water.

A cool, crystal-clear stream flowed through the subterranean room. Fish were swimming in the water, and their sleek bodies flashed over a golden, glittering river bottom. *The river was flowing over a bed of gold!*

His heart pounding, Dorr scooped up a handful of nuggets and inspected them carefully under the lamp. This was no fool's gold. This was a true bonanza. Wealth beyond his most frustrated and impatient dreams lay on the floor of the river.

The prospector followed the stream through the length of the room. The riverbanks were embedded with gold, and somewhere along the stream's course lay the real mother lode.

Then Dorr made his most important discovery. Investigating the walls of the room, he found thick, rich veins of gold running

through the quartz structure. Many students of lost treasures believe that the grizzled old prospector stood in the very heart of one of the world's richest gold deposits.

With trembling hands, Dorr stuffed his pockets with nuggets and flakes of gold and headed for the surface. As he retraced the strange, twisting route, he marked the cave wall for future trips.

Outside the cave, barely daring to believe the size of his find, Dorr erected a hasty claim marker, then drove to the Barstow courthouse to file an official claim on the property.

At the courthouse, Dorr was stunned to learn that the property had already been marked and claimed by another prospector who believed the possibility of a rich mineral strike centered around the *entrance to the cave.*

Disillusioned, yet unwilling to jump another man's claim, Earl Dorr mentally retraced his trip into the cave. There was a possibility—admittedly a slim one—that the underground room and river lay beneath *unclaimed* land. Dorr hurried back to the cave to test his theory, stopping only to purchase dynamite, a compass, and pencil and paper.

Back in the cave, he tabulated the direction, distance, and depth of each turn in the madcap, tortuous route. Several pages of complicated directions had been compiled by the time he reached the golden river.

Dorr gazed in wonder at the riches within the vault and sighed. In Barstow, Earl Dorr was well known for his unwavering honesty and his strict ethical principles. Claim-jumping was definitely against the moral code of the desert treasure-hunter, and his pockets were empty when he left the rich underground room.

Dorr used the dynamite to blast shut the small tunnel entrance to the underground river. When the dust and debris settled, he used the flame of his carbide lamp to write D-O-R-R across the pile of rock and dirt.

The penciled figures on his sheets of paper led the prospector to a desert area near Highway 91, just east of Windmill station. He retraced the route several times to verify his conclusions.

It was here, at last, that Dorr filed his claim, supposedly directly

over the underground room with its golden river. He constructed a work shack and began to sink a shaft into the sandy desert earth.

Months passed, and then years. The depression of the 1930s arrived and departed while Earl Dorr continued to sink useless hole after hole into the charred, dry earth. His only reward was sweat, sand, and searing sun. Whenever his spirits sagged, however, he would recall the fantastic nugget-rich river of gold somewhere beneath the surface.

One afternoon, after he had struck moist earth, Dorr unearthed several human bones and a skull. An anthropologist from a nearby university theorized that, centuries ago, the bones had been left after some ritual had been held by Indians on the riverbanks when the stream ran on what was then the surface.

A geologist mused that it was quite possible that ancient Indians had used the underground river for transportation through the desert and mountains: "They might have ridden logs through the underground waters of the stream, and possibly some were caught in the tomblike caverns."

Dorr visualized the hapless Indian unable to escape from the cavern, eventually starving to death, his bones perserved until he had dug them up.

At least such theories reaffirmed his own account of the underground river, but the genial prospector was never to return to his legendary stream of gold. He died with only his golden memories in 1958. The lost river of gold in the desert is still lost.

# CHAPTER NINETEEN

# GHOSTS WALK THE STREETS OF JEROME, THE WICKEDEST CITY IN THE WEST

Jerome, Arizona, sits on a 30 degree mountainside 2,000 feet above the picturesque Verde Valley. It is not really fair to call it a ghost town, in the usual sense of the term, even though the Phelps Dodge Corporation shut down the copper mines in 1953, and the population soon dropped to around 120. At its peak in the 1920s, the "billion dollar copper camp" supported a citizenry of 15,000. Today, there are around 470 folks who maintain an artists' colony, operate art galleries, run antique shops, host colorful restaurants and bars, and staff a number of museums that preserve former glories.

As a Western buff, Brad was surprised to learn that the copper deposits were discovered by General Crook's famous Indian guide, Al Sieber. Known by the Apache as a "man of iron," because of his legendary powers of endurance, Sieber was also wise in the ways of metallurgy and he recognized the potential of the copper in this Arizona mountainside. The rugged scout actually filed the first claim to the ore in 1876.

In one of those strange quirks of fate, Sieber never made a cent out of his discovery, but he passed on a tip about the area to a couple of enterprising fellows named Angus McKinnon and M. A. Ruffner, who took the tough scout at his word and began the work that would lead to the eventual excavation of eight hundred billion dollars worth of copper from Jerome.

The town was named for a New York City financier who never even visited the place. In 1882, Eugene Murray Jerome said that he would invest some badly needed capital in the mining claims, provided that the camp be named after him. Eugene's only other claim to fame lay in the fact that he was a cousin of Jennie Jerome, Sir Winston Churchill's mother.

For seventy-seven years, men worked the mines in Jerome, carving out an amazing eighty-seven miles of tunnels under the town. And in those nearly eight decades, there were a lot of accidents, deaths on the job, and miners dying of lung problems.

Today, it is the number of spirits walking the streets that make Jerome a ghost town, not its lack of human occupants.

As we drove up Highway 89A from the Verde Valley, we had a strong sense of leaving the present behind and driving into a dimension of reality apart from contemporary time. Old gasoline signs, antiquated posters for forgotten brands of soft drinks, the prevalent turn-of-the century architecture of the store fronts on main street, and the houses stacked on the hillside created a time warp that made it seem as if we were back in an earlier decade of this century.

The mine museum and gift shop occupies a building that was originally constructed in 1898 to house an elegant saloon. We decided to begin our nosing about for tales of Jerome's restless spirits amidst the artifacts of mining days past.

A good many stories centered about the United Verde Hospital that sits high on Cleopatra Hill. In its day, it must have been quite an impressive building of tile, cement, and lots of glass windows. It was used to treat miners from 1927 to 1951.

A young man who had worked in the library for a time told us of being in the old hospital after dark one night and hearing the sounds of coughing, labored breathing, together with moans and cries of pain.

"I know that a lot of miners developed lung problems from their work," he said, "and I think I heard the ghostly sounds of men suf-

fering from that terrible occupational hazard."

It seems that certain of the local artists like to paint in the old building, making good use of the light from its many windows. We heard that several painters had reported weird occurrences while working on their canvases.

"There's ghostly energy all over that old hospital," one of them stated. "If you want to work in there, you just have to get used to it. You make your peace with the spirits. They won't hurt you. They're just people, after all."

Another artist swore that his hair literally stood on end when he felt a powerful "zap" from a ghost he encountered in the hospital. "I had bad dreams about the ghost for weeks after that. The experience really shook me up."

❖

There is another, older hospital farther down on Cleopatra Hill where manifestations have also been reported.

"One night when I was walking by the place, I suddenly felt an incredible energy coming from the building," a young woman told us. "Someone had told me that the ghosts in Jerome came out stronger when there was a full moon and a low-pressure system. I didn't know about the low-pressure system, but there was a full moon that night.

"I don't know why I decided to walk into the place. I can only explain that I was drawn to do so, as if something was telling me that I needed to have a certain kind of experience for my spiritual growth," she continued.

"At first I heard the sounds of people breathing heavily, then I could hear sighs and moans. I had a flashlight with me, but I felt that I should not turn it on. Enough moonlight was filtering in for me to see pretty clearly.

"Then I saw the dim shapes of several bodies lying covered with blankets in a hallway. I could see doctors and nurses rushing around the bodies, bending over them. The whole scene only lasted about ten or twelve seconds, then it was gone.

"I knew that there had been accidents in the mines, and so forth,

but when I did some research on the history of Jerome, I read about the awful influenza epidemic that struck around 1917 and '18 and I had an inner knowing that I was seeing a scene from that terrible time."

Quite a few Jerome residents know about the ghost of "Headless Charlie," the spirit of a miner who was decapitated in a grisly mine accident. According to legend, Charlie's head was found in the bottom of the shaft, but his body was never recovered.

"Old Charlie had really big feet," we were told, "and not long after he got his head chopped off, the miners started finding these big footprints in the mine. It's said that Headless Charlie still walks around down there in the tunnels."

Not far from Spook Hall, the one-time dance hall and current community center and spook convention headquarters, is the area where the "cribs" were located. Although these crude shacks and rough buildings have been torn down, they once housed the "working girls," the ladies of the evening in Jerome's red-light area.

"The story goes that a couple of miners got into a fight over this prostitute, who ended up getting in the middle of the struggle and getting knifed," a Jerome old-timer told us. "I don't know why her particular ghost appears out of so many hookers that got beat up or killed here, but lots of folks claim to see her walk from the spot where the cribs were up to a few feet from the Little Daisy Hotel, then disappear. It seems more people see her when the moon is full."

Some years ago, Brad became friends with a former Phoenix fireman named Bill Finch, who was an accomplished metaphysician. Before his death, Bill had retired to the Cottonwood-Sedona area and begun a small, but extremely productive, publishing company.

Bill and his daughter, Lana Ivie, had even reprinted a couple of Brad's older books.

Brad recalled that for a time Lana had published a historical monthly entitled the *Jerome Ghost Post*. It had been Lana's theory that Jerome had so many ghosts because it had experienced an "overabundance of violent deaths" during its heyday. Her research through old newspaper files demonstrated to her that there had been many deaths in the town due to stabbings, gunshot wounds, and mining accidents.

Lana believed, as did her father, that certain people are more sensitive to ghostly phenomena than others. "It may be similar to musical or artistic ability," she mused. "Some people are just more sensitive to the presence of ghosts."

❖

One longtime resident confessed that she had been a skeptic and a doubter when she had first heard some of the ghost tales of Jerome.

"I became a believer when I had a personal encounter of my own," she told us. "Initially, it was just an energy I felt in my room. Then I came face to face with the ghosts of a miner and his lady of the evening sitting on a sofa in my living room. Now I sleep with the night-light on!"

❖

Before we left Jerome, the tough little mining town that had once earned the title of the "wickedest city in the West," Sherry felt compelled to climb Cleopatra Hill once more and to train her camera on a building near the old Episcopal church.

When the developed film was returned, she saw what appears to be a ghostly figure in the doorway. We may have brought home our own spook from Jerome.

# CHAPTER TWENTY

# TUCSON'S MYSTERY CROSSES AND FORGOTTEN MINES OF INCREDIBLE ANTIQUITY IN UTAH AND OKLAHOMA

**E**vidence of an unknown civilization that existed on the North American continent continues to surface and baffle the experts, and nowhere have more mysterious artifacts been found than in the Southwest.

On September 13, 1924, near Tucson, Arizona, Charles E. Manier found the first of what would prove to be a series of unusual objects inscribed in a language that resembles, but clearly isn't, Latin. Among the twenty-seven artifacts eventually discovered are six crosses, nine swords or sword fragments, a spear-headed serpent cross, and a crescent cross.

According to some authorities, the language inscribed on the artifacts appears to be Latin of a style popular up to A.D. 900, and dates on some of the pieces would seem to bear out this supposition. However, a few Hebrew words thrown in here and there add to the confusion when it comes to establishing a clear cultural attribution for the artifacts. It all becomes a complete historical puzzler when the inscriptions attempt to record a journal of settlement and exploration.

One theory is that a band of explorers, perhaps from the Mediterranean area, with a knowledge of Christian symbolism and the Latin and Hebrew languages, somehow, about A.D. 800, managed to get themselves to the American Southwest. Here, nearly

seven hundred years before Columbus' voyage of discovery, they established a colony, recorded their history, and then proceeded to pass into obscurity.

Some of the Hebrew words found jumbled in with the Latin are those for *Jehovah*, *Peace*, and *Mighty Empire*. Among the many questions raised by such inscriptions are whether the unknown explorers considered *themselves* representatives of a mighty empire or whether they found themselves confronted with the hordes of a mighty empire in the American Southwest.

Certain researchers have been bold enough to suggest that the language on the artifacts is not really Latin at all, but the language of a "mighty empire" that once existed in the American Southwest.

In other words, the inscriptions on the objects found near Tucson may have many of the same characters and perhaps a good many cognates of Latin as we know it, for the basic reason that the mighty empire in the Southwest existed thousands of years ago on this continent and was actually the culture that seeded the Mediterranean. To say it all another way, the Old World is really the New World and vice versa.

Even so, some skeptics maintain that the mysterious crosses and swords with their peculiar Latin inscriptions could all be the result of some ambitious and incredible hoax.

In 1953 miners of the Lion coal mine of Wattis, Utah, broke into a mysterious network of tunnels between five and six feet in height and width that contained previously mined coal of such vast antiquity that it had become weathered to a state of uselessness for any kind of burning or heat. A search outside the mountain in direct line with the tunnels revealed no sign of any entrance. Since the tunnels were discovered when the miners were working an eight-foot coal seam at eighty-five hundred feet, the evidence strongly suggests that miners from some unknown civilization conducted an ambitious mining project so far back in time that all exterior traces have been eroded away.

The February 1954 issue of *Coal Age* quoted Professor John E.

Wilson of the department of engineering of the University of Utah in regard to the mystery mines of Wattis:

"Without a doubt, both drifts were man-made. Though no evidence was found at the outcrop, the tunnels apparently were driven some 450 feet from the outside to the point where the present workings broke into them.... There is no visible basis for dating the tunnels."

Jesse D. Jennings, professor of anthropology at the University of Utah, said that while he was unable to name the identity of the ancient miners, he knew that the vast tunnels and coal-mining rooms were definitely not the work of any American Indian people. Such a vast mining network would have required an immediate and local need for coal, and Professor Jennings pointed out, "There is no reported extensive burning of coal by aboriginals in the region of the Wattis mine."

❖

In private correspondence, W. W. McCormick of Abilene, Texas, relates his grandfather's account of a strange building of an unknown civilization that was found buried in a coal-mine shaft:

"In the year 1928, I, A. A. Mathis, was working in coal mine No. 5, located two miles north of Heavener, Oklahoma. This was a shaft mine, and they told us it was two miles deep. The mine was so deep that they let us down into it on an elevator.... They pumped air down to us, it was so deep.

"One night I shot four shots [referring to the charges used to blast the coal loose] in room 24 of this mine, and the next morning there were several concrete blocks laying in the room. These blocks were 12-inch cubes and were so smooth and polished on the outside that all six sides could serve as mirrors. Yet they were full of gravel, because I chipped one of them open with my pick, and it was plain concrete inside.

"As I started to timber the room up, it caved in—and I barely escaped. When I came back after the cave-in, a solid wall of these polished blocks was left exposed. About 100 to 150 yards farther

down our air core, another miner struck this same wall—or one very similar.

"Immediately, [the mining company officers] pulled us out of this wing and forbade us to tell anything we had seen.

"The mine was closed in the fall of 1928, and the crew went to Kentucky.

"Before I started working on this crew, they had a similar experience in mine 24 at Wilburton, Oklahoma in about the year 1926. They said they dug up two odd things: One was a solid block of silver in the shape of a barrel, and the other was a bone that was about the size of an elephant's leg bone.

"The silver block had the imprints of the staves on it, and the saw that first struck it cut off a chip on the edge of one end. The miners saw the silver dust the saw was pulling out and went back to dig out the block.

"What was done with these things, I do not know. In the case of the blocks in my room in No. 5, I don't think any were kept."

And what of the weird discoveries rumored to be found in the Wilburton mines?

Wilbert H. Rusch, Sr., professor of biology at Concordia College in Ann Arbor, quoted a letter a colleague had received from Frank J. Kenwood, who said that he had been a fireman in the Municipal Electric Plant in Thomas, Oklahoma, in 1912, when he split a large piece of coal and discovered an iron pot encased within.

"This iron pot fell from the center, leaving the impression or mould of the pot in the piece of coal," Kenwood wrote. "I traced the source of the coal, and found that it had come from the Wilburton, Oklahoma, mines."

***Phantom Hitchhiker****. On a lonely stretch of highway between California and Arizona a ghostly hitchhiker seems to be trying to flag someone down. There are hundreds of reports of these apparitions on Southwest highways—day and night. (Photo credit: Sherry Hansen-Steiger)*

***Apache Ceremonial Dancers****. While many Southwest Native American dances re-create or reenact important events, such as this one of the hunt, others simulate natural phenomena such as the movement of the stars. Many tribes were taught by the Ancient Ones that the purpose of dance is to keep a harmony and balance with the Earth Mother and with body, mind, and spirit of all living creatures. Each tribe has its unique drumbeat and rhythm of dances that balance Mother Earth's sacred energy points. (Photo credit: Sherry Hansen-Steiger)*

**The Wickedest City.** *A historic mining town of the Southwest, Jerome, Arizona, was at one time one of the richest in the world. Jerome yielded a bonanza of copper, gold, silver, zinc, and lead during its active seventy-seven years of mining—totaling a billion dollars. Now Jerome boasts of having once been the "wickedest city" in the West. (Photo credit: Sherry Hansen-Steiger)*

**Montezuma's Well.** *Located just six miles north of Montezuma's Castle, Montezuma's Well is part of the same monument. Only 470 feet in diameter, this is one of the most unusual geological spots in the Southwest. This spring-fed limestone sink supplies a thousand gallons of water per minute and one and one-half million gallons a day. This area is thought to have been inhabited by the Hohokum Indians in the seventh century A.D. and then by the Sinaguas ("without water"), who must have been ecstatic to come upon this magical well. Note the ruins in the caves at the upper left corner. (Photo credit: Sherry Hansen-Steiger)*

**Montezuma Castle National Monument.** *The first settlers to see this impressive fortress in northern Arizona considered it of Aztec origin and so named it after the great Montezuma. (Photo credit: Sherry Hansen-Steiger)*

**Montezuma Castle.** *The Anasazi (Sinagua) Indians simply vanished from this and the surrounding sites, perhaps because of illness or disputes. While it is not known for sure what drove them away from this protected paradise, some speculate that a bizarre fire might have chased them out, never to return. Note the charred ceiling of the cave. (Photo credit: Sherry Hansen-Steiger)*

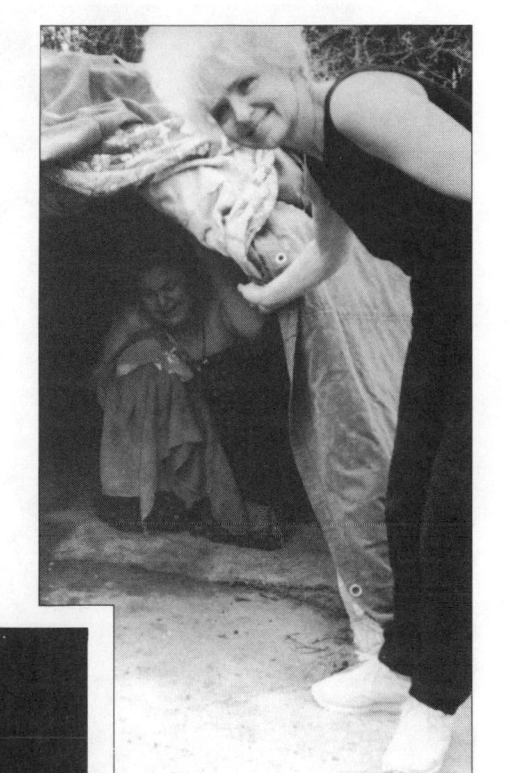

*Jo Ann Parks, keeper of the Texas Crystal Skull affectionately known as "Max," holds open the entrance as Mary Thunder emerges. Mary and Max held council and did the ceremony in the sacred sweat.*

*"Max" is one of the thirteen known human-sized crystal skulls in the world. Here, with a photograph of the total solar eclipse behind her, Mary Thunder, in symbolic gesture, conducts a ceremony of total alignment utilizing Max's energy to balance mind, body, and spirit.*

*Author Brad Steiger points to the city of Sedona, Arizona, below, as he discusses the theory that this area is a dimensional doorway enabling telepathic communication and attracting UFOs. (Photo credit: Sherry Hansen-Steiger)*

**Cathedral Rock.** *Like a king on a throne, this energy vortex reveals the beauty of the red rock with a mane of greenery all around. Many of those interviewed by the authors stated their belief that the entire area of Sedona is a vortex, and that there is no discernible difference between the various vortex spots. The red rocks are highly piezoelectric, with a strong iron content. Could there be a scientific explanation for the mystical experiences so many people have had here? (Photo credit: Sherry Hansen-Steiger)*

*The Chapel of the Holy Cross not only provides one of the most spectacular views of Sedona but also seems to be the spot that attracts so many people psychically. Many report having visions or memories of temples and caves here, perhaps from the time of Atlantis. (Photo credit: Sherry Hansen-Steiger)*

*Sherry Hansen-Steiger is unknowingly photographed as she meditates on a ledge in Sedona. This series of three pictures shows what appear to be balls of energy coming in and intensifying until Sherry is immersed in a beam of light. Sherry has described the energy she experiences in a deep state of meditation as an electromagnetic tube of light protecting her. Note the little fairy angel/butterfly in the upper right-hand corner of the third photograph. The Butterfly Center for Transformation is a school she founded in the 1970s. This is not trick photography—not even a special lens was used. (Photo courtesy Timothy Beckley)*

**The Gathering of the Eagles.** *"Our work seems to be revolving around the 'space people,' and the need to awaken those starpeople to their own innate talents to better themselves and the planet," say Jean and Luis Romero as they stand in front of their popular art. (Photo credit: Sherry Hansen-Steiger)*

**Petroglyph.** *An ancient petroglyph found in Colorado depicts what appears to be space beings with antennae on their heads. Note the domelike space craft behind them, resting on a tripod. Nearly all Native Americans have legends of skypeople who are their ancestors. (Photo courtesy F. Michael Mola)*

*An 1850 Catholic cemetery in Old Town, San Diego, where many historic people are buried—but are they at rest? There are numerous reports of ghostly sightings here. Father Lazarus, the church historian, points to the stone wall around the cemetery and to the house next door as he tells the authors about the poltergeist disturbances that drove the neighbors to have the area exorcised. (Photo credit: Sherry Hansen-Steiger)*

**El Fandango.** *Stories abound about the woman in white with a hazy, nebulous appearance who sits at a corner table in the window of the El Fandango Restaurant in Old Town, San Diego. The identity of the lady in the window is currently being researched. A similar apparition has been sighted at the Whaley house, the Estudillo, and other places in the area. (Photo credit: Sherry Hansen-Steiger)*

*The Robinson–Rose house was the first commercial structure in San Diego as well as home to the Robinsons, who built it in 1853. Many ghosts frequent this place, which is now the park's visitor center. (Photo credit: Sherry Hansen-Steiger)*

*The Whaley House Museum is one of thirty ghost houses listed by the U.S. Department of Commerce, and one of two in California. At least four spirits are frequently seen in the Whaley house and are assumed to be from the family that built the house in 1856. (Photo credit: Sherry Hansen-Steiger)*

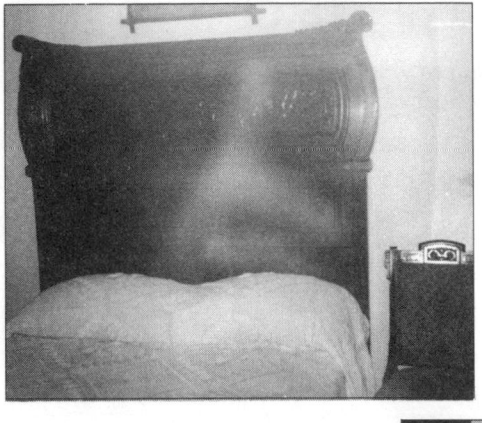

*The Whaley House. A ghostly entity appears to be stuck getting up on the wrong side of the bed. (Photo courtesy Doreen Turner)*

*A wide range of ghostly manifestations frequents the Whaley house, including cooking odors, the smell of Mr. Whaley's favorite Cuban cigar, Mrs. Whaley's perfume, and even chains swinging by themselves as though there is a child swinging on them. Here it almost looks as if someone is trying to use the old spinning wheel. Is it possible that the family is not even aware that they have passed on? (Photo courtesy Doreen Turner)*

*Grandmother Twylah with Brad and Sherry Steiger. Twylah Nitsch is the Repositor of Seneca Wisdom.*

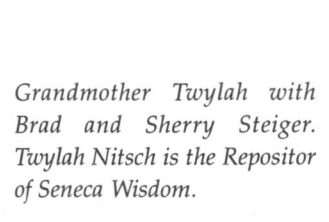

# CHAPTER TWENTY-ONE

# THE ELEPHANTS OF NEW MEXICO

About 1910 a small boy playing in the tiny settlement of Flora Vista, New Mexico, dug up two slabs of carved rock and uncovered a controversy that has raged ever since.

What the unsuspecting lad presented to the scientific world on those strange rock slabs was, first of all, a number of symbols of an ancient language that no one could decipher. Secondly, petroglyphs (rock drawings) of easily recognizable local indigenous animals— *and two elephants.*

Elephants—complete with trunks and floppy ears and tusks.

The boy found the slabs in eight-hundred-year-old Indian ruins on the Animas River, opposite the village of Flora Vista.

Is it possible for someone to draw a picture of an elephant without ever have seen one?

And, more specifically, was it possible for an ancient Native American to have sat on a bank of the Animas and accidentally, by chance, have etched the image of an elephant on stone?

You have quite likely heard the old anecdote illustrating the laws of probability which postulates that if you put enough monkeys in a room with enough typewriters and enough paper, one of them will type out the "To be or not to be" soliloquy from *Hamlet.*

Do the same laws of probability apply to countless ancient American artists? If enough of them sat carving petroglyphs of

known animals, might one of them just happen to make a creative leap and randomly reproduce the image of an elephant?

Alternative explanations might include the following:

1. Artistic representations of African elephants found their way to ancient New Mexico via the trade ships of Phoenicians between 900 and 200 B.C.

2. The memory of the great woolly mammoths had been preserved by the Indians' oral tradition or by representations of the great beasts made by even more ancient artists.

3. An Asiatic potentate launched an invasion fleet, complete with war elephants, to colonize the New World. Many scholarly researchers have suggested that the ancient Chinese could well have reached the west coasts of the Americas. If such an invasion did take place in historical times, the native dwellers would certainly have been impressed by the giant mammals and would have surely captured the beasts' likeness for posterity.

Then, of course, we must always entertain the dour possibility that the elephant slabs of Flora Vista are the work of a hoaxster who hid his fakes in the old ruins and patiently awaited their discovery by an archaeologist—or a small boy.

# CHAPTER TWENTY-TWO

# MYSTERY WALLS IN TEXAS, OKLAHOMA, AND CALIFORNIA

On November 5, 1967, Frank Tolbert, columnist for the Dallas *Morning News*, wrote about a buried city under Rockwall, Texas. According to Tolbert, the most long-lasting and persistent argument in Rockwall, the smallest county in Texas, revolved around whether or not four of its 147 square miles supported the great stone walls of an ancient fortification (some of which reached heights of forty-nine feet) or if, as most geologists insisted, the walls were but "nature's masonry in the shape of sandstone dikes."

Raymond B. Cameron once told Tolbert that the walls of the mystery city were about eight inches thick and that the stones had been formed, or placed, on top of each other with the ends breaking near the center of the stone above or below, just as a fine mason would build a wall. The stones gave the appearance of having been beveled around their edges, and the walls were too regular in appearance to have been formed by nature.

Cameron went on to say that there was a mortarlike substance between the stones. Then he dropped his biggest blockbuster:

"Four large stones taken from wall segments appear to have been inscribed by some form of writing. This couldn't have been done by erosion, since the stones were underground."

Tolbert also recalled the visit of a famous archaeologist, Count Byron Kuhn de Porok, to Dallas in the 1920s: "The count seemed to

lean heavily on the theory that these were once the walls of an ancient city. He said the walls looked remarkably like those of buried cities that he had excavated in North Africa and the Middle East."

On June 27, 1969, workmen leveling a rock shelf at 122nd Street on the Broadway extension between Edmond and Oklahoma City, Oklahoma, uncovered a rock formation that looked just like an inlaid mosaic tile floor.

"I am sure this was man-made because the stones are placed in perfect sets of parallel lines which intersect to form a diamond shape all pointing to the east," said Durwood Pate, an Oklahoma City geologist who studied the site and who was quoted in the Edmond *Booster*, July 3, 1969:

"We found post holes which measure a perfect two rods from the other two. The top of the stone is very smooth, and if you lift one of them, you will find that it is very jagged, which indicates wear on the surface. Everything is too well placed to be a natural formation."

Delbert Smith, a geologist, president of the Oklahoma Seismograph Company, said the formation, which was discovered about three feet beneath the surface, appeared to cover several thousand square feet. On June 29, 1969, Smith told the Tulsa *World*, "There is no question about it. It has been laid there, but I have no idea by whom."

Neither does anyone have any idea who constructed the mysterious walls that run for seven miles through the Berkeley and Oakland, California, hills.

The rather ordinary-looking stone walls are found mainly in heavily wooded or chaparral-covered areas. Although in a few places it appears as if they might have been used as some kind of fortification, they seem to fulfill none of the usual functions of walls.

According to the research of Sibley S. Morrill, the walls survive in sections ranging from twenty feet to more than two hundred yards in length. In height they vary from two feet or less to five feet or a bit more. Their breadth at ground level is a quite impressive four feet. In Morrill's opinion, such breadth would seem to indicate "that the walls originally were much higher through the use of smaller stones along the top."

Limited digging near the base indicates that the rock goes down about ten inches below the surface. It is difficult to imagine the wall having been built just for fun, since some of the rocks employed in its construction weigh more than two hundred pounds.

Seth Simpson of Oakland is said to have studied the walls as a hobby for a good many years. He followed the walls for nearly seven miles south into the Oakland hills, but he was unable to relate them to any known boundary markings.

"Water-company survey maps show that none of these walls have any detectable relationship to boundary lines. Except for one case in the Vollmer Peak area," Simpson said, "boundary lines parallel no walls nearer than about six hundred yards."

Neither does any clue remain to suggest that the walls might be the remnants of any sort of animal pen or corral.

Morrill found the walls to be, for the most part, straight. "Some intersect at an angle," he said, "and there are instances of parallel walls separated by as much as ten yards or so; but there are no indications whatever that they ever formed enclosures."

In the hills behind Milpitas, Simpson discovered similar walls in a gently rolling, almost treeless country. Once again, he could detect none of the usual purposes for building a wall. Virtually useless as fences, the stone walls just "run their way for a few score or few hundred yards and then stop."

No area resident appears to know anything about the origins of the walls. They have just always been there.

# CHAPTER TWENTY-THREE

# IMPOSSIBLE FOOTPRINTS IN THE STONES OF THE SOUTHWEST

According to the accepted academic calendars of time, an early ancestor of man is supposed to have evolved in the late Tertiary period, indicating that mankind is only about one million years old. However, across the Southwestern states of Nevada, Utah, Oklahoma, and Texas fossilized footprints of bare and shod feet of something that appears decidedly human have been found impressed in rocks from the Carboniferous period to the Cambrian period, thus offering mute but dramatic testimony that some bipedal creature—very, very humanlike—was walking about from 250 to 500 million years ago.

Although the discovery of these footprints in the stones of time are hardly rare or recent occurrences, geologists by and large refuse to accept such fossil evidence at face value because to do so would be to acknowledge that modern man lived in the earliest years of hypothetical evolutionary history.

Albert C. Ingalls, writing of such footprints, labeled them the "carboniferous mystery" in *Scientific American,* January 1940: "If man, or even his ape ancestor, or even that ape ancestor's early mammalian ancestor, existed as far back as in the Carboniferous Period in any shape then the whole science of geology is so completely wrong that all the geologists will resign their jobs and take up truck driving. Hence for the present at least, science rejects the

attractive explanation that [human feet] made these mysterious prints in the mud of the Carboniferous Period...."

Well, then, if not humans, who—or what—was walking around leaving human footprints millions and millions of years ago?

On January 25, 1927, while hiking in Nevada, a Mr. Knapp discovered a shoesole that was fossilized in Triassic limestone—thereby placing humans back in the time of the giant reptiles. Knapp said that the fossil lay among some loose rocks.

He picked it up, and upon closer examination, "came to the conclusion that it is a layer from the heel of a shoe which had been pulled from the balance of the heel by suction; the rock being in a plastic state at that time.

"I found it in limestone of the Triassic Period," he said, "a belt of which runs through that section of the hills."

The relic was taken to New York, where it was analyzed by a competent geologist of the Rockefeller Foundation, who verified Knapp's assessment and pronounced the fossil as unquestionably from Triassic limestone.

"Micro-photographs were made which showed very clearly that [the fossil] bore a minute resemblance to a well-made piece of leather, stitched by hand and at one time worn by a human foot," stated the geologist's report. "The [micro-photographs] showed the stitches very plainly; at one place it was double-stitched and the twist of the thread could be clearly seen. The thread is smaller than any used by shoemakers of today...."

Samuel Hubbard, honorary curator of archaeology of the Oakland, California, Museum, examined the curious find and said, "There are whole races of primitive men on earth today, utterly incapable of...sewing that moccasin. What becomes of the Darwinian Theory in the face of this evidence that there were intelligent men on earth millions of years before apes are supposed to have evolved?"

✜

The White Sands National Monument near Alamogordo, New Mexico, contains some 176,000 acres of white alabaster. Geologists

theorize that this gypsum was precipitated as arid winds dried up an inland sea. Somewhere in the great expanse of gypsum are what appear to be the sandal prints of some prehistoric human giant, who could only have made such impressions when the muddy sediment of the primeval ocean was beginning to harden.

In the *"Story of the Great White Sands,"* a booklet distributed at the national monument, there appears an account concerning the discovery of the massive human tracks:

"In the fall of 1932, Ellis Wright, a government trapper, reported that he had found human tracks of unbelievable size imprinted in the gypsum rock on the west side of White Sands....

"As Mr. Wright reported, there were thirteen human tracks... each [one] approximately 22 inches long and from eight-to-ten inches wide. It was the consensus [of the investigating group] that the tracks were made by a human being, for the print was perfect, and even the instep plainly marked. However, there was no one in the group who cared to venture a guess as to when the tracks were made, or how they came to be of their tremendous size. It is one of the great unsolved mysteries of the Great White Sands."

In her "Happenings—Past and Present" column in the Silver City *Enterprise*, April 1, 1971, Mary Wright told of a group of people who had contacted a national monument ranger for a tour of the area in which Ellis Wright [apparently no relation to Mary] had found the gigantic tracks of prehistoric humans. Allegedly, additional imprints in the gypsum had been discovered:

"Since these tracks, which were in hardened caliche, were twice the size of [contemporary humans], who were these early day travelers and what could they have been seeking in the San Andreas mountains? They were wearing some type of sandal or moccasin. They crossed these lakes when the caliche was soft, as their tracks show."

On May 25, 1969, the Tulsa *Sunday World* carried an article

describing the fossilized footprints found by Troy Johnson, a North American Rockwell liaison engineer. Amazingly, just a few miles from Tulsa's eastern city limits, Johnson removed earth, roots, and stone from an outcropping of sandstone to reveal animal prints—many off which he could not identify—and some distinctive, five-toed, humanlike footprints.

"The chunk of sandstone containing the big prints is a massive weight of an estimated 15 tons, which rules out the possibility of someone transporting it to the top of the hill," Johnson said. "Also, the stone is of the same strata as other specimens of sandstone dotting the hilltop, indicating that there was a monumental 'uplift' of the earth's crust ages ago."

Dr. Clifford Burdick, an expert geologist from Tucson, Arizona, spent more than thirty years studying what appear to be human footprints in strata contemporaneous with dinosaur tracks. His extensive investigation of the several imprints found at Glen Rose, Texas, has convinced him that they are authentic human footprints.

Dr. Burdick's examination of the "footprints in stone" began in the early 1950s when the Natural Science Foundation of Los Angeles assigned him to accompany four other scientists to investigate the reported man-tracks that had been found in strata contemporaneous with dinosaur prints in and around Glen Rose, Texas. The Natural Science Foundation committee soon learned that local residents had been cutting dinosaur and human tracks out of the limestone of the Paluxy riverbed near Glen Rose since at least 1938. A Mr. Berry gave them an affidavit which stated that in September of that year, he and other men found "many dinosaur tracks, several sabre-tooth tiger tracks, and three human tracks" in the riverbed.

The committee soon met Jim Ryals, who had dug up and sold dozens of tracks from the Paluxy River area. Ryals informed them that lots of folks thereabout had been selling the tracks during hard times so that tourist dollars could help them through the Depression. To add to the committee's despair that so many specimens had already been chipped out and sold off, Ryals said that

because of the prints' curiosity value, some less-principled individuals in the area had taken to carving man-tracks and dinosaur prints of their own.

"The way to tell the difference," Ryals explained, "is to look for the ridges around the tracks. Those are pressure ridges that were formed around the footprints by the displacement of mud. If the tracks have pressure ridges, then they are genuine. As you can see, those tracks found by Mr. Berry definitely have pressure ridges."

Dr. Burdick learned that Dr. Roland Bird, field explorer for the American Museum of Natural History of New York City, had also examined the tracks found by Berry, and he had described them in the May 1939 edition of *Natural History magazine.*

Dr. Bird admitted that he had never seen anything like the tracks, and he assessed them as "perfect in every detail." But since the manlike tracks measured sixteen inches from toe to heel, he declared that they were too large to be human—although the barefoot tracks did show all the toes, insteps, and heels in the proper proportions.

Jim Ryals had accompanied Dr. Bird when he made a special field trip to the Paluxy River to examine the tracks in place. The scientist had become less enthusiastic about the footprints when he saw them in association with dinosaur tracks, because "humans did not live in the age of dinosaurs." So his trip would not be a total waste, Dr. Bird dug up several large Brontosaurus tracks and shipped them to the museum.

Dr. Burdick became very excited about the find of Charles Moss, who discovered a series of nearly twenty perfect giant barefoot human tracks, each about sixteen inches in length and eight inches in width.

"The stride was about six feet until the fellow started to run," Dr. Burdick commented. "Then the stride lengthened to nine feet, when only the balls of the feet showed, with the toes. Then the series disappeared into the bank."

The challenge offered by these remarkable footprints in the Paluxy riverbed require a meaningful scientific explanation. Whatever species of creature made these tracks, it was definitely

bipedal. The footprints all have about the same length of stride, which would be consistent with a human with a sixteen-inch foot.

The shapes of the prints are certainly more humanlike than any other animal known to science. If the prints are accepted as being human, scientists will be forced either to place man back in time to the Cretaceous period or to bring the dinosaurs forward to the Pleistocene or Recent period.

Frank X. Tolbert has written about the alleged man-tracks in the Paluxy River for years in his column in the Dallas *Morning News*. Although he has been consistently skeptical toward any allegations that the tracks were actually those of ancient humans, in his January 6, 1973, column, Tolbert wrote of a remarkably clear find of the footprint of a "huge humanoid" that measured twenty-one and a half inches in length, eight inches in width across the front of the foot, and five and one-half inches across the instep.

Dr. C. N. Dougherty of Glen Rose stated that the footprint was found near the deeply engraved prints of three-toed dinosaurs. "These man-tracks belong to the Mesozoic Era," Dr. Dougherty said, "because the clearest one is exactly eight inches from a trachodon track and on the same layer of rock. The trachodon tracks are as clear and distinct as the man-track."

Tolbert explained in his column that seeking out the man-tracks and the dinosaur impressions in the Paluxy riverbed is arduous work. First of all, one has to wait for the arid seasons when the river has no moving water and the waterfall has gone temporarily dry. Dr. Dougherty admitted that he had swept a big stretch of the riverbed during the time of drought before he found that "best of all tracks."

"When I discovered this trail of a giant man under the waterfall, I had a feeling that it was one of the most important discoveries since the Dead Sea Scolls and what is believed to be Noah's Ark on Mount Ararat," Dr. Dougherty said.

In referring to the evidence of the Glen Rose, Texas, tracks, Dr. Burdick stated that the general theory of evolution would be dealt a lethal blow, because the geologic record of human footprints contemporaneous with dinosaur tracks "suggests that simple and complex types of life were coexistent in time past or during geologic ages.... This does not harmonize with the hypothesis that complex types of life evolved from lower or more simple forms."

The theory of evolution implies that through the geologic ages life has not only become more complex, but it has also increased in size. "If evidence from the man-tracks can be used as a criterion," Dr. Burdick pointed out in his *Footprints in the Sands of Time*, "ancient man was much larger than modern man as an average. This harmonized with most fossil life which was larger than its modern counterpart.... On the whole, biological life has had to contend with unfavorable environment, which has been a factor in its degeneration, rather than its evolution."

❖

In July 1968 William Meister, an amateur rockhound, made a discovery that most certainly does not harmonize with the accepted theories of evolution. While searching for fossils at Antelope Springs, near Delta, Utah, Meister unearthed what appears to be a fossilized human sandal print with a trilobite, an extinct marine animal, imbedded in the impression made by the heel.

Since the impression was made on what once may have been a sandy beach during the Cambrian period of the Paleozoic Era, the sandal print would have to be an incredible *five hundred million years old*.

Dr. Burdick personally investigated Meister's find, and while digging in the same area where the rockhound had found the remarkable sandal print, he himself was fortunate enough to find "on a slab of shale the impression of a child's bare foot with all five toes showing dimly."

A few days later, Dr. Burdick found a human track similar to the one Meister had discovered, "evidently made by shoes or moccasins." According to Burdick, professors of the geological depart-

ment of a leading university agreed that the tracks definitely looked human, but they could not accept their apparent biological origins.

Dr. Burdick stressed to his academic colleagues the point that the tracks with human appearance had been preserved in rock hundreds of feet below the present surface of the ground. "If these are verified as human tracks, the discovery will have far-reaching repercussions throughout the scientific world," he said.

"Cambrian fossils, such as trilobites, are placed at the bottom of Paleozoic, some estimated 600 million years before man evolved, according to evolutionary geology. This evidence, if verified, will practically collapse the geologic column."

# CHAPTER TWENTY-FOUR

# MYSTERY MUMMIES AND SKELETONS OF A CIVILIZATION OF GIANTS

In 1898, H. Flagler Cowden and his brother Charles C. Cowden, scientists who had dedicated themselves to the study of desert antiquity, were conducting an archaeological dig in desolate Death Valley. It was here that they uncovered the skeletal remains of a human being believed to be the largest and oldest ever found in the United States.

The fossilized human remains were those of a giant female, seven and a half feet tall, and the Cowdens stated their theory that she had been a member of "the race of unprecedented large primitives which vanished from the face of the earth some 100,000 years ago." Although turn-of-the century scientists did not have our modern carbon-dating methods of determining the antiquity of an object, the Cowdens were able to reach their conclusions of time and age by the amount of silica in the soil and sands and by the state of petrification of the skeleton, along with the crystallization and opalization of the bone marrow.

Ed Earl Repp, a writer, told of the "honor and privilege" that were his in working with the Cowden brothers; in the June 1970 issue of *Wild West* magazine he recalled that "in the same earth strata where the giant female skeleton was found, they also recovered the remains of prehistoric camels and mammals of…an elephantlike creature with four tusks…. With them were the remains

of petrified palm trees, towering ferns, and prehistoric fishlike creatures."

The Cowdens theorized that in times of vast antiquity when the lost race of giants lived there, Death Valley may have been an inlet of the Pacific Ocean, for in the same pit in which they found the skeleton of the giant female they also unearthed the petrified remains of marine life.

The two brothers also found that the giant woman's skeleton bore a number of anomalous physical appendages and attributes not found in contemporary humans. The existence of several extra "buttons" at the base of the woman's spine indicated that she and her people were endowed with tails. They also discovered that her canine teeth were twice the length of modern humans.'

The Cowdens theorized that when the California we know today was formed, together with the rising of mountains and the retreat of the seas, the tropical climate left the valley regions. The steaming swamps were replaced by vast wastelands, which still remain over much of the southern portion of the state.

The fossilized remains of the seven-and-a-half-foot woman were found at a depth of five feet in a "hard-rock formation of conglomerate containing small amounts of silica, which required longer time to petrify than normal desert sands."

Perhaps prehistoric California was the original home of the Amazons, those legendary, statuesque female warriors; in July 1895 a party of miners working near Bridlevale Falls found the tomb of a woman whose skeletal remains indicated that she had stood six feet, eight inches.

G. F. Martindale, who was in charge of the miners, noticed a pile of stones that seemed to have been placed against the wall of a cliff in an unnatural formation. Assuming that the rock had been stacked by human hands, Martindale ordered his men to begin removing the stones in order to investigate what might lie beyond the formation.

The miners were astonished when they found a wall of rock that

had been shaped and fitted together with apparent knowledge of fine masonry technique. Convinced that they had stumbled upon some lost treasure trove, they set about tearing down the wall so that they might claim their riches.

Instead of ingots of gold or trunks of jewels, the men found a mummified corpse of a very large woman lying on a ledge that had been carved from natural stone. The corpse had been wrapped in animal skins and covered with a very fine powder. She was clutching a child to her breast.

When the mummy was taken to Los Angeles, scientists agreed that the woman was a member of a giant race that had thrived on this continent long before the American Indian had become the dominant inhabitant. They concluded that the mummy's height of six feet, eight inches would have represented a height in life of at least seven feet. Figuring the classic height difference between men and women, they supposed that the males of the forgotten species would have been nearly eight feet tall.

On July 30, 1974, the indefatigable Frank X. Tolbert reported in the Dallas *Morning News* that the skeletal remains of a seven-foot woman had been found sealed in a cave at the crest of a high mesa near the small town of Chalk Mountain. The final resting place of the giant woman had been discovered by Dr. Ernest Adams, an amateur archaeologist.

Dr. Adams set forth his theory that the woman had been of average size for her unknown race and that "the cave was a maternity ward for these giants...the cave was steam-heated by water boiled under the floor...the woman had died in childbirth, apparently. And her perfect teeth suggested that she was quite young."

Explorers of the back country and archaeologists keep coming up with strong indications that a much larger race inhabited the American Southwest in prehistoric times. Harold T. Wilkins discovered a petroglyph in Supai Canyon, Arizona, that depicts a mam-

moth attacking a human. According to the perspective employed by the ancient artist, Wilkins estimated that the beleaguered man must have been over ten feet tall. Indians in the vicinity stated that the drawings had been made by the "giants of long ago."

A skull found in one of the many cliff dwellings near Winslow, Arizona, was described by Jesse J. Benton in his *Cow by the Tail* as being so large that a cowboy's Stetson sat on it "like one of those tiny hats merrymakers wear on New Year's." Benton also stated that a gold tooth had been found in the skull, thereby ruling out the likelihood of the headbone having once been connected to a giant animal rather than a giant human.

*The New York Times* on December 2, 1930, carried an item that told of the discovery of the remains of an apparent race of giants who once lived at Sayopa, Sonora, a mining town three hundred miles south of the Mexican border. J. E. Coker, a mining engineer, stated that laborers clearing ranchland near the Yazui River had dug into a very old cemetery and had found "bodies of men, averaging eight feet in height, buried tier by tier."

Indeed, in those ancient days, there were giants on the Earth.

# CHAPTER TWENTY-FIVE

# WEREANIMALS THAT STALK NAVAJO COUNTRY

David Little Turtle told us of the Navajo shepherd near Window Rock, Arizona, who was out hunting one night with the goal of thinning down the coyote population that had been carrying off his sheep. He caught a glimpse of a large coyote running behind a clump of mesquite, and he walked around the bush with his rifle at the ready.

"Don't shoot, Brother!" shouted a female voice. "You will kill a member of your own clan."

The shepherd was astonished when the coyote pulled back its skin to reveal a woman he recognized as one of his cousins.

"I will conduct a powerful sing for you, Brother," she told him. "And you will say nothing of this to anyone."

The shepherd nodded his head in silent agreement. He had long suspected his kinswoman of being a witch, but to see her in the act of transforming herself into a coyote had made him feel as though his brain were afloat in tequila.

Once the witch sensed that she had his true vow of secrecy, she slipped the coyote skin back over her head and ran off with such speed that she became but a blur of motion.

"The Navajo believe in wereanimals," David Little Turtle said.

"This woman probably kept the skin of the coyote hidden some-where in a cave or in her home. When she wanted to join with other witches or to move about at night with great speed, she would put on the magic skin.

"Other witches might keep the hide of a bear, a fox, a wolf, or a mountain lion hidden away for such purposes of night travel. Together, in caves and other secret meeting places, the witches gather to plot against their enemies, to initiate new members, sometimes to eat human flesh or to have sexual intercourse with corpses."

✤

"The werecreatures in which the Navajos believe are not quite the same as, for example, the popular werewolf of European tradi-tions," a Native American psychiatrist in Phoenix explained. "Interestingly, though, it is the wolfmen who are most common in America as in Europe, but the creatures are supernatural beings that take the shape of men or women and—at will—can travel many, many miles in the blink of an eye and appear as wolves or as men dressing in wolf's clothing."

An attractive young Navajo woman, a secretarial worker in Phoenix and a convert to Roman Catholicism, told us of the experi-ence that her brother had undergone while hitchhiking to their grandmother's home late one night.

"It was in February and it was pretty cold. It was past midnight, and he just couldn't go any farther. There are these little bus stops on the roads where they pick up schoolchildren, so he was sitting there, debating whether or not to spend the night in there or to keep walking the second half of the fifty miles to Grandmother's home.

"Then he saw this animal. He thought it was a dog. He wanted some company so he whistled at it. It came running right by him and they scared each other. The 'dog' stood up on its hind legs. My brother said it had a man's face, and the face was painted with lit-tle white dots and other kinds of signs. It had on an animal's skin. The thing ran off on four legs, and my brother tried to run after it, but it was too fast.

"My brother said that it dawned on him then what he had seen. He had never really believed in things like that until then. He said that he guessed it was true that medicine people really have the power to travel in such a way.

"In other words, medicine people have the power to travel long distances in no time at all in the form of a wolf. During the time that they are traveling in this fashion, they are not supposed to talk to anybody until they reach their destination.

"My brother did not tell our grandmother about the incident until several months later; because if he had, Grandmother would have become excited, and she would have said that we would have to have a sing to chase the evil spirits away. When he told us about his experience, it made us wonder about it."

❖

A Navajo named Manuel told us about his grandfather's experience with two witches who could transform their bodies into cats. Or perhaps it was the other way around.

"Grandfather did not know that these two sisters were witches. He was but a boy of fifteen then, and not nearly so wise as when he was an old man," Manuel explained. "He could not as quickly recognize the sign of wereanimals."

Manuel's grandfather, Esteban, had grown up in a village not far from the Arizona–New Mexico border. One day while he was herding his father's sheep, he came upon a small hut in which two sisters, Isabel and Carmelita, lived alone. On their first meeting, they had been very courteous to him, and had given him some cool water and some Indian fry bread.*

Isabel seemed to be Esteban's own age, and Carmelita appeared to be only a few years older. Since they were pretty girls and there was little to do in the evenings in the small village, the young man began to slip out at night to visit them.

Although Esteban thought it strange for two single girls to live alone and apart from the village, he did not discuss the matter with

---

* An unleavened bread fried in oil.

his parents, because he was certain that they would forbid him to make his nocturnal calls to the mysterious sisters. Esteban found Isabel and Carmelita far and away the most exciting things in his life, and he would not do anything that might jeopardize his growing relationship with his newfound friends. He told no one, not even his closest companions, about the two sisters.

Esteban, Isabel, and Carmelita would play cards and laugh at their own jokes. The sisters made good food for him, and they gave him something to drink that tasted somewhat bitter but that made him feel warm and happy. Carmelita played the guitar, and the two sisters knew many songs that Esteban had never heard anywhere else. They sang of medicine people with great powers, of witches and sorcerors, of the great Montezuma and the serpent of wisdom.

Esteban cherished the hours with Carmelita and Isabel, and each night he was saddened when it was time for him to run across the moonlit rocks to his parents' home. He would silently slip into the hogan and into his bedroll, very careful to wake no one.

Soon Carmelita began to ask Esteban to stay until after midnight. "If you would not run off to your father's house, you could stay and have some real fun with us," she teased him. "We would show you things such as you have never dreamed of."

Carmelita's tongue reached out to moisten her full, red lips, and Esteban became excited by the very invitation, which his adolescent hormones took to be one of sexual promise. He would run home across the rough rocks almost trembling with frustration and thwarted desire.

At last came the day when Esteban could think of nothing but the two beautiful sisters. He had never had a woman, and thoughts of his two full-bodied friends with their long black hair and smoldering brown eyes were nearly driving him to stumble over cliffs. If several hungry coyotes would have come that day to carry off sheep, it is doubtful if Esteban would even have noticed their presence or their gory deeds.

He did, in fact, become so careless in his preoccupation that five sheep wandered off and became lost.

Esteban's father was furious, and the young man, to save face,

vowed that he would not return home until he had all five of the missing sheep following him to the night pens.

Somehow, he managed to fulfill his vow through the good graces of his keen senses, and he brought each of the five strays home to the pens. Although he knew it had to be nearly midnight, he took time only for a couple of mouthfuls of fry bread and beans, and he set out for the hut of Isabel and Carmelita.

His common sense told him that he was doing a foolish, perhaps even discourteous thing. Isabel and Carmelita might be sleeping, and they could feel insulted by his boldness.

On the other hand, the girls certainly implied that they stayed up most of the night, laughing, playing the guitar, singing. And on many occasions Carmelita had certainly led him to believe that she wished him to stay the night with them.

Esteban was disappointed when he pushed open the door of the small hut. Carmelita and Isabel were gone. Their dwelling place was empty except for half a dozen large cats that began to yowl at him the moment that he set foot inside the home.

"How did you damn things get in here?" he wondered aloud.

Carmelita and Isabel kept no animals. These cats had to be wild, homeless strays that had been attracted to the house by the domestic odors of cooking. He had, in fact, interrupted their feasting from two pans of food that the sisters must have left on the floor.

Esteban called the girls' names, hoping they might be somewhere outside. Only the screeching cats answered his plaintive summons.

Esteban felt himself becoming hot-faced with frustration and rage. In his disgust, he kicked the largest cat—the one that had been rubbing itself against his leg ever since he had arrived at the hut. The cat howled its pain as it sailed across the room and crashed into a large metal frying pan. When it lifted its head to glare at Esteban, blood was running over its face.

The young man left the hut feeling somewhat sheepish that he had taken out his anger on the cat, but his guilt was soon dissipated when he felt sharp fangs pierce his right ankle. One of the other cats had sought vengeance and was biting him. As he reached

down to scoop the vicious creature away, another cat bit him on his hand.

Esteban had had enough. His disappointment at being cheated out of an imagined night of love combined with his fury at being bitten by the strange cats that had mysteriously appeared in Isabel's and Carmelita's hut. He pried open the cat's jaw that was gnawing at his ankle, seized the little beast by its back legs and dashed its brains out against a rock. The cat that had bitten his hand managed to escape only after Esteban had landed a solid kick that must have broken a few ribs.

The next evening Esteban called upon the two sisters to inquire of them where they had been the night before. An angry, hostile Carmelita met him at the door and told him that he was no longer welcome in their home.

Although she wore a shawl, Esteban could see that her head was bandaged. Directly behind her were the shadowy figures of four older women who glared at him with hatred such as he had never before perceived.

"If you are looking for Isabel," one of the crones hissed at him. "She lies buried out back. She was killed last night when she fell and struck her head on a rock."

Esteban's senses began to whirl. His ankle began to throb anew with pain as he recalled the large cat that had sunk its fangs so deeply into his flesh before he dashed its brains out against a rock.

"Begone!" shouted another of the old women. "Begone before we—"

Her threat was interrupted by a fit of coughing, and when she straightened up again, blood was mixed with the spittle running down her chin. It seemed apparent from the manner in which she moved that she had several broken ribs.

Esteban would never forget Carmelita's parting words or the smile that revealed long, catlike fangs: "If only you would have stayed after midnight some night, Esteban, we could have had such a good time."

Manuel said that his grandfather later confessed the entire experience to his father, who immediately ordered a sing to purify

Esteban and to drive away the influence of any evil that might have lingered near him in spirit form.

A few months later, Esteban heard a familiar voice singing in the village marketplace. He knew at once that it was Carmelita. As he cautiously approached the woman and the crowd that had gathered to listen to the eerie words of the strange song, he was astonished to see before him the figure of a very old woman.

"At first Grandfather thought that he must have been mistaken, that it was just an old woman that happened to know the same weird songs that Carmelita had sung," Manuel said. "But as he drew nearer, he could see the still-vivid scar on her head from the wound that she had received when he had thrown her cat-body against the frying pan. Grandfather felt frightened anew, for then he realized that the youth and the beauty of Carmelita and Isabel had also been illusions. They had been wrinkled old crones all along."

# CHAPTER TWENTY-SIX

# HAUNTED HOTELS OF THE SOUTHWEST

In 1990, Bill Gilbert, a twenty-two-year veteran of the San Francisco police force, bought Brookdale Lodge, a sprawling old resort that had been built in 1924 in the Santa Cruz Mountains near Boulder Creek, California.

Gilbert knew that the colorful inn, which features a brook running through the dining room, had been a popular hideaway for Mafia kingpins in the 1930s and 1940s. He was also aware that such Hollywood film legends as Marilyn Monroe, Joan Crawford, and Tyrone Power had made the place one of their favorite retreats. What Gilbert did not quite understand when he bought the place was that Brookdale Lodge is haunted.

Perhaps at first it might have seemed to Gilbert as though the doors that slammed shut for no apparent reason and the strange "cold spots" that chilled various areas of the lodge during hot summer days all went with the secret tunnels and hidden rooms of the old resort. But when television sets, ice machines, and jukeboxes began to turn on and off by themselves, it occurred to the ex-cop that along with the resort, he had purchased the ghosts of certain guests who had never checked out.

Then there was the gardenialike fragrance that seemed to follow some people around and came to upset certain guests. There was also the Mermaid Room that would, on occasion, echo with eerie

big-band music from the 1940s and the sounds of people laughing, dancing, and clinking glasses.

Late one October night in 1990, around 2:30 A.M., Gilbert's twenty-four-year-old daughter Kim was sitting in the cocktail lounge talking with one of the waitresses when she saw the figure of a child she assumed to be her four-year-old daughter, Melanie, running through the lobby. Understandably concerned for her daughter's well-being, Kim went upstairs to check on her.

"I found that both doors leading upstairs were locked," Kim said, "and there was no way Melanie could have opened them without a key. When I got upstairs, she was sound asleep."

Later, after comparing impressions with the waitress, Kim concluded that they had not seen a small girl in her nightie run across the lobby, but a little girl dressed very formally in 1940s-style clothing. A bit of research among the area residents turned up the local legend that the ghost was that of Sarah, the five-year-old niece of the lodge's original owner. Sometime in the late 1940s, Sarah had drowned in the indoor-portion of the creek that runs through the hotel.

Kim referred to one particular staircase that Melanie was terrified to use. The stairway leads from the Pool Room down to the Mermaid Room, and Melanie begged her mother not to make her go down there.

Kim called in two Gnostic ministers to perform a "house blessing" on Brookdale Lodge, and the Gilberts have also sought the impressions of well-known psychic sensitive Sylvia Browne of Campbell, California.

Commenting to the press on her two visits to Brookdale Lodge, Browne stated: "That place is really ominous. It sent chills up my spine the moment I walked in the door."

❖

"I was awakened in the middle of the night by the sounds of a man clearing his throat," said a woman who was telling us about the strange occurrence she witnessed in the Hotel Monte Vista in Flagstaff, Arizona. "I opened one eye at the disturbance, then again

heard the sound of a man clearing his throat in a kind of nervous, upset manner."

Logically assuming the noises to be issuing from her husband, she opened both eyes to see him pacing back and forth across the hotel room in a state of obvious agitation. "Honey, what is wrong?" she asked, concerned. "What's the matter?"

A grunt beside her redirected her consciousness to the fact that her husband lay sleeping beside her in bed. "Nothing's wrong," he said into his pillow. "I'm trying to sleep."

"And then I saw clearly that the man who was pacing the floor in such a state of nervousness was most certainly not my husband," she said. "I sat up in bed, about to ask him who in the blazes he was, when he vanished right before my eyes."

✛

The picturesque old Monte Vista Hotel provides a marvelous place for an overnight stay on the way to or from the Grand Canyon. According to some guests, it may also provide an encounter with the unknown.

One guest told of his strange interaction with what he termed "the phantom bellboy." It seemed that he was plagued throughout the night by a brisk knocking on his door, followed by a muffled voice saying, "Room service!" Whenever he would sleepily stagger out of bed to answer the door, there would no one in sight.

"Yeah, I know," he said defensively. "People are going to say that someone was just playing a trick on me. But that hallway was a long one, and if it were a jokester, he would really have to make tracks quickly. And silently, or I would at least have heard him running away.

"This happened at least six times during the night," he continued. "Sure, it took me longer each time to open the door, but the first few times when I was up watching television, I was at the door in seconds. I'm convinced it was some kind of ghost."

Another person, a traveling saleswoman who had stayed at the Monte Vista on several occasions, said that she was certain that she had seen the wispy image of a woman standing poised to knock

just outside of the Zane Grey room. "Maybe I can't prove to the skeptical that the ghost wasn't just the result of fatigue or some kind of trick of the light," she said. "But I will always know what I saw there."

Fans of Zane Grey's Westerns may have read of the Monte Visa under its original name, the Community Hotel, in many of the author's novels. In fact, Grey put up the initial one hundred thousand dollars to get the place built back in 1927.

A Western enthusiast from back East purposely requested the Zane Grey Suite, the largest of the hotel's eleven suites. "I just felt as though I could sense the essence of the great novelist as he sat working on an adventure set under the Tonto Rim or somewhere amidst the purple sage," he said.

There is no reason to question the tourist's romantic inclinations, but "sensing" the essence of an author who probably never wrote a sentence in the suite named for him does not receive the same rating on the supernatural scoreboard as actually seeing a ghost.

Such Hollywood stars as Humphrey Bogart, Clark Gable, John Wayne, Walter Brennan, and Alan Ladd also stayed at the Monte Vista, but we have not heard any accounts of anyone having encountered one of their spirits treading the plush carpets of the hotel.

There are said to be so many ghosts at the historic old Horton Grand Hotel in San Diego that the specters often get together and hold dances.

Shelly Deegan said that she lived in the hotel for two years. Once when she was walking up the spiral staircase to the third floor, she came upon a group of fifteen to twenty men and women, all seemingly in a very festive mood.

"They were all dressed in the style of the 1890s," she said, "and they were having a dance."

It was only after she had watched them for a time that Shelly

realized that there was something very strange about the scene. No one paid the slightest attention to her. Everyone appeared to ignore her when she spoke.

Then it struck her that the costumes were just too perfect, the dance, just too stylized and precise. And there was something very eerie about their eyes, kind of hollow and dark. She knew then that the men and women were really ghosts.

For some reason, Shelly stated, the ghostly figures had not disappeared at the intrusion of her human presence. It seemed as though they were permitting her to observe the incredible manifestation of what may have been a recreation of some past scene that had once occurred in the hotel.

They swung their partners round and round, she said. "I could even hear the flute music. They seemed to be having a great time."

For generations now, guests have been claiming ghostly encounters at the old San Diego hotel. Perhaps the room that receives the most nominations as "most haunted" is number 309. It was in this room that a gambler named Roger Whittaker was murdered for his money more than one hundred years ago.

Dan Pearson, the owner of the Horton Grand, said that he first became aware that there were "problems" with the room when he brought a crew in to renovate the place in 1986. As Pearson walked by Room 309 with a friend who was psychically talented, the man stopped suddenly and said: "There's something going on in that room! I feel it strongly!"

Pearson said that three months later, a guest at the hotel found her young daughter carrying on an animated conversation with someone in the room. Since the mother could see only her daughter, she could not avoid asking her little girl to whom she was speaking.

Her daughter looked up incredulously. "Don't you see him, Mommy? Don't you see the man in our room?"

Although Shelly Deegan was a witness to a ballroom full of dancing ghosts, she never saw the image of Roger Whittaker in the two years that she stayed at the Horton Grand Hotel. She did sense his presence, though.

"I once asked Roger to give me a signal that he was there," Shelly said. "A few minutes later I was stunned to see the clear imprint of a man's body on the bed. It seems Roger had lain down to show me that he was around."

A traveling salesman from New Jersey who was staying at the old San Carlos Hotel in Phoenix complained to the front desk about the noisy children in the next room who were preventing him from taking a much-needed nap. When he was informed that there was no one in the rooms on either side of him and no children anywhere on his floor, he became outraged that his word was questioned. Those shouting, squealing, laughing kids had been driving him crazy.

Leaving his room to give the desk clerk a piece of his angry mind and, if necessary, to drag him upstairs to hear the racket for himself, the salesman opened the door to spot three young boys running down the hallway. The salesman set out in earnest pursuit of the youngsters, fully intending to scoop up at least one of the boys to present as evidence of the boisterous kids who were disturbing his rest.

"I nearly had one of the little buggers when the kid and his two buddies disappeared right in front of me," the man said. "I don't mean they turned a sudden corner and got away. I mean they just completely vanished into thin air."

Later, while he was getting a drink at a nearby bar to settle his nerves, the elderly bartender told him that the old San Carlos had been built sometime in the late 1920s on the site of Phoenix's first adobe elementary school.

"Life was hard in old Arizona," the bartender told him. "Maybe you saw the ghosts of some schoolkids who died before they got to finish school. Maybe they were just trying to find the old schoolhouse."

# CHAPTER TWENTY-SEVEN

# THE ANCIENT RUINS OF LOST TRIBES

In the minds of the orthodox archaeologist and anthropologist, the origins of the American Indian have been clearly charted: Sporadic migrations of Asiatic peoples crossed from Siberia into Alaska over a period of fifteen thousand years or more. In other words, in the scenario the academicians have constructed for us, we are to believe that before the Siberians invaded the New World, the continents were like the Garden of Eden without an Adam or an Eve.

But the anomalous Amerindian blood type and their unique dental composition, plus the geographic distribution of the various tribes, would all demand an impossible genetic timetable in which to transform the Asiatic invaders into the distinctive New World citizens that Columbus and the early Spanish invaders christened Indians. Even if we were to attempt to keep some kind of peace with the accepted theories of New World habitation, we must grant more evolution in forty thousand years in North America than that which occurred in more than a million years in Europe, Africa, and Asia. And as a final staggering punch, the case for immigrating Asiatics arriving to populate North and South America approximately fifteen thousand years ago seems completely discredited by the fifty-thousand-year-old skulls found in California that are clearly those of American Indians.

Most of the traditional American Indians with whom we have discussed the question of the origins of their people on the continents of North and South America simply do not accept the Bering Strait-invasion hypothesis as the complete account of their genesis. They do not deny that such a Mongolian invasion took place any more than they deny that the European invasion occurred, but they do not believe that the origins of the Amerindian are to be found in Siberia any more than they are to be discovered in England or France.

The physical makeup of certain tribes, especially those of the far Northwest, bear mute testimony that interbreeding occurred between Amerindian and Asiatic ethnic groups, just as many tribes bear evidence of interbreeding with European ethnic groups. But the traditional Amerindian stoutly insists that just as there were tribespeople on the shore to welcome the European to North America, so were various tribes already on this continent to host the Siberian immigrants.

The traditional people believe that they are the descendants of those who survived the destruction of a great civilization that once existed on this continent. And the medicine priests and traditional people believed this long before the sleeping prophet Edgar Cayce declared that the ancient inhabitants of lost Atlantis were a red-skinned people. What is more, today numerous medicine priests are speaking out and revealing that the true home of the Amerindian people, the garden that seeded Atlantis, was in the stars, specifically the Pleiades.

For one thing, the medicine priests point out, the ancient people who came over from Siberia were very primitive. How then, utilizing the orthodox timetable, does the anthropologist explain the sophisticated stone tools found in an ancient Mexican streambed which were considerably more advanced than those used in Europe and Asia 250,000 years ago? The most primitive tools found in the streambed were of a type used in the Old World thirty-five thousand to forty thousand years ago.

Of the startling discovery, Dr. Ronald Frywell of Washington State University told *The New York Times* (November 18, 1973): "We

have apparently found geological data that led to a head-on confrontation with apparently sound archaeological data."

✜

Corn, that marvelously versatile New World contribution to the pantries of the planet, is said to be, at nine thousand years, our oldest domesticated seed crop. Therefore, some early agriculturalist had to be on this continent more than nine thousand years ago in order to domesticate the seed. However, conclusive proof that skilled farmers were harvesting corn *long before* 7,000 B.C. was obtained when a Humble Oil Company drill brought up Mexican corn pollen that was more than eighty thousand years old.

✜

And equally dramatic as finding sophisticated stone tools 250,000 years old and corn pollen 80,000 years old are the discovery of the many strange walled cities and fortifications that have been found scattered through the Southwest and other parts of the United States. As we discussed in Chapter Twenty-four, the ruins are of vast antiquity and their skilled masons remain completely anonymous.

✜

Rabbinical literature states that "worlds upon worlds there were—before Adam was." Many of those researchers who seek to unlock the secrets of the past have begun to suspect that many times before our present Earth age, untold civilizations were buried as the planet was created, leveled, and re-created again and again.

Each of the Amerindian tribes with which we are familiar cherishes legends that tell of their people rising from the destruction that had been visited upon a former civilization. The principal point of these myths of destruction and rebirth is that civilization is cyclical, continually being born, struggling toward a golden age, then slipping backward in moral morass into its death throes, only to be reborn so that the process may begin once more.

The vast majority of the ancient texts of Europe and Asia deal specifically with the recurrence of catastrophes. The Old Testament records disasters in which mountains melt like wax, seas are parted, and people are swallowed up by the earth or charred to cinders by fire and brimstone from above.

Perhaps, as some saddened philosophers have observed, humankind is the victim of some kind of collective amnesia, forced to undergo certain traumatic experiences over and over again.

For the Amerindian traditionalist, the destructions of the previous "worlds" have been a necessary part of humankind's spiritual evolution. Because we humans repeatedly forget the lessons of the Great Mystery, the Earth Mother has periodically cleansed herself in order to begin new epochs purified and refreshed.

## Montezuma's Well and Castle

Although we have discussed the reverence the various Southwestern tribes hold for Montezuma, it was early Anglo settlers and soldiers who named the ancient Arizona ruins Montezuma Castle and Montezuma Well after the legendary Aztec emperor.

Centuries before Montezuma ruled the great Aztec empire, a people known today as the Sinagua [Spanish for "without water"] farmed simple crops in the Verde Valley and built the impressive cliff dwellings at the Castle and the stone village at Tuzigoot. Scholars still debate both the origins of the Sinagua and the reason for their disappearance sometime around the 1400s.

Both the Sinagua and the Hohokam irrigated their crops from the Montezuma Well, which qualifies as one of the unusual geological spots in the Southwest. The well is actually a limestone sink formed eons ago by the collapse of an enormous underground cavern. A million and a half gallons of water per day flow from underground springs to fill a deep round cavity atop a hill. The well is truly a remarkable oasis that rises high above the surrounding desert.

## THE BIG HOUSE AT CASA GRANDE
## AND OTHER ANCIENT OBSERVATORIES

In the mid-1970s, John P. Molloy of the University of Arizona suggested that ancient Mayas may have used the Caracol Tower at Chichén Itzá as an astronomical observatory. Furthermore, he theorized that the astronomers of Caracol could have established a network of pre-Conquest observatories that may have extended throughout significant sites in Central and North America. In pursuit of his theory, Molloy has also searched for astronomically significant alignments at the Big House, Casa Grande National Monument, near Coolidge, Arizona. This area was inhabited by the Hohokam Indians from 200 B.C. to A.D. 1475. The Big House itself was probably in use from A.D. 900 to 1100.

In the June 1976 issue of *Sky and Telescope*, Robert D. Hicks III writes that the Big House "is a three-story rectangular building of caliche and adobe, set upon a one-story platform substructure. The symmetrical plan contains five contiguous room tiers, four of which rise two stories and surround a central three-story tier. Astronomically significant alignments are found for windows and holes in the second-story west wall and for the third-story walls."

Molloy's theory holds that the various alignment holes all have lines of sight to the horizon and give the appearance of having been placed with great care. Of the fourteen openings investigated, eight were found to be celestially aligned, basically to the Sun and Moon, with the solstices and equinoxes indicated.

"Two sets of openings, Holes 6 and 7, are located directly above 8 and 9, all giving eastern horizon positions," Hicks states in his article. "This redundancy provided for 'fine tuning.'"

Molloy's research appears to have demonstrated numerous affinities between the Big House in Arizona and the Caracol Tower "observatory" in Yucatán, Mexico. Such study, Hicks points out, will undoubtedly provide "new insights into the ancient American past" and demonstrate the establishment of pre-Columbian astronomy.

Jonathan Reyman of Illinois State University investigated astro-

nomical alignments at various sites in the area of Chaco Canyon, New Mexico. A number of solstitial markers were tentatively identified by this astroarchaeologist.

Warren L. Wittry has described an astronomical observing station at Cahokia [circa A.D. 1000], a large Indian settlement in what is now St. Louis, Missouri. Called the American Woodhenge because of its superficial resemblance to the European henge stone monuments, the largest circle consisted of forty-eight wooden posts, the arc between each of them being seven and one-half degrees, while an additional post was approximately five feet east of the true center.

It seemed evident to Wittry and other investigators that from the post east of true center one would have been able to look due east in line with a post on the circle and witness sunrise at the equinoxes. In addition, from the same off-center post, one could look past the fourth post north or south of due east to observe the sunrise at the summer and winter solstices.

## SPIRIT MANIFESTATIONS AT THE RUINS

The anthropological and archaeological mysteries of these ruins are a challenge to science and a wonder for the layman to consider. But their often eerie appearance holds more than enigmas for scholars. There are strange occurrences taking place at many of these ancient ruins.

Marsha, formerly a guide for one of the jeep tours in the Sedona area, told us of her encounter with the unseen dimension:

"There are many ruins around here, Hopi, Navajo, Sinagua, and so forth," she said. "There is one ruin that we believe was something like a monastery where medicine priests from many ancient tribes gathered. One day just at sunset, I went there with my friend Jamie, whom I had been promising for months to show the ruins. It was so quiet and peaceful without a jeep full of tourists asking me a hundred and one questions.

"But as it got darker, we heard drumming and singing. I said to Jamie, 'Oh, no, kid, we're not alone after all.' A lot of people

around here are really into the American Indian mystique, so I figured some group was up in the ruins holding some kind of ceremony or other.

"Jamie and I were walking very carefully, so as not to fall over a cliff—and very quietly, so as not to disturb the group that was drumming and chanting," Marsha said. "We could smell smoke from their fire, and I thought that was not very smart, to build a fire in the ruins, and all.

"I was just wondering whether to interrupt them and bawl them out for being irresponsible with the fire when we came around a corner of one of the old houses to see probably a dozen or more old Indian men seated around a fire. Their outfits looked so authentic and they were singing so earnestly that Jamie and I just stood there spellbound.

"We didn't stand there immobile for very long, though," Marsha said. "For in the next few seconds, the whole group of drumming, chanting Indian men began to fade away. Jamie clutched at my arm, and I saw that her eyes were wide with a mixture of fear and awe. I guess I was feeling that same combination of emotions as we both comprehended that we were observing either a group of ghosts or a scene from the past. Within, I would say, half a minute, the entire scene had completely vanished."

A man who had served in the information center at Montezuma Castle for many years told us that whenever he went out along Beaver Creek and looked up at the magnificent cliff dwellings that had been fashioned hundreds of years ago by the vanished Sinagua people, he felt a presence near him.

"I more or less began to identify with the ancient Sinagua," Mel told us. "I could visualize myself carrying water up to one of the rooms in the dwellings that I felt was mine. I could see myself working in the gardens that sustained the community. And always I could feel this presence beside me, friendly, totally nonthreatening. I could even say that I felt love emanating to me from this invisible being."

✛

Charmaine Yarune Boericke, a psychic-sensitive, shared an account of a spiritual visit to a "magical healing" canyon that she is convinced also exists in the physical dimension near one of the ruins in the Sedona area.

"One night when I was very ill and making all kinds of prayers and supplications to the inner teachers and my guardian angel, an American Indian suddenly appeared beside my bed," Charmaine said. "I called him Blue Feather, because hanging down behind his left ear was one single blue feather about five inches long.

"As he stood beside my bed, I realized that he had come in answer to my supplications, so I told him about my trouble and how I had a pain that I simply could not stand any longer—and I thanked him for coming to help me."

The next thing that Charmaine knew, she was with Blue Feather in a canyon somewhere. The spirit healer seated her on a rock.

"It was very, very comfortable," Charmaine recalled. "And the canyon seemed so very familiar to me. Blue Feather called in his spirit helpers, who gathered rocks and built a circle of them, making me a part of the circle. Blue Feather rubbed red clay between his palms, then mixed it with something that he took from a little pouch inside his belt. He made a paste of the mixture and rubbed it into my forehead."

Throughout his preparation of the paste, Blue Feather had been chanting, praying, calling out, and going through certain ritualistic motions. Charmaine was astonished to see that he could light magical fires simply by asking for them. Soon, he was blowing the smoke from the fires directly at Charmaine.

"I'm afraid that I wasn't thinking very spiritual thoughts," she admitted. "I questioned whether or not the heavy smoke would choke me."

When Blue Feather had completed the ceremony, Charmaine found herself once again back in her own bed. "I was totally well, and I have never suffered from that problem again."

Charmaine stated that the entity known to her as Blue Feather

159

has been a very significant factor in her life. "But he does not come to me in times of mere stress and strain," she said. "He only comes to me when it is a matter of life and death."

"This used to bother me a little. I used to wonder why I couldn't get help whenever I needed it. Now I realize that we humans must learn to get ourselves together and to get ourselves out of our own problems."

✜

Sandra Escobar said that she had been sitting on one of the park benches overlooking the Montezuma Well when she found unusual thoughts coming to her from "out of nowhere." Sandra emphasized to us that she is a bank teller in Prescott, Arizona, and she is not "into" New Age things, such as channeling spirit entities.

"I just felt love moving over me," she said. "I literally felt as though I were one with the universe. I was the cloud in the sky, the ant at my feet, the ducks on the lake in the Montezuma Well. I was one with everything.

"Then I heard this voice speaking to me inside my head," she continued. 'Don't be afraid, Sister,' it said in a tone that was neither really male or female. 'Love this land, love this earth, love your time as we did our time. Care for your world as we cared for ours. Don't let the Greedy Ones, the Careless Ones, the Ones Without Heart destroy our Mother.'"

Sandy is convinced that she received a personal message to become more concerned about ecological causes. "I know the 'mother' the voice referred to is Mother Earth. Humankind has treated her so badly, I want to do whatever I can to help atone for the sins that we have committed against her. I want to revere the Earth Mother the way the ancient Indians did."

## "Max," the Incredible Ten-Thousand-Year-Old Crystal Skull

Jo Ann and Carl Parks became the owners of the famous Texas Crystal Skull, whom they affectionately call Max, when a Tibetan

healer bestowed the artifact on them in payment of a debt. Admittedly unaware at first of the remarkable qualities of this object, Carl and Jo Ann, residents of Houston, placed the skull in a closet for the next seven years.

Not until they came into contact with F. R. "Nick" Nocerino of Pinole, California, the world's foremost authority on crystal skulls, did Jo Ann and Carl learn what a truly important artifact rested in obscurity in their closet. Nocerino had been searching for that very skull since the 1940s. He knew of its existence, but its actual location had sent him on a quest that had led him around the world.

Carl and Jo Ann state that it was a very "happy day for all of us" when they were finally brought together with Nocerino, founder and director of the Society of Crystal Skulls. Now, after the proper authentication and research has been completed, Carl and Jo Ann can begin to appreciate the crystal skull of which they are caretakers.

They learned that there are only thirteen crystal skulls known to researchers that are the actual true size of a human head. Of those known to the Society of Crystal Skulls, Max is the largest, weighing eighteen pounds compared to the others, which weigh nine to eleven pounds. Other than Max and the crystal skull owned by Anna Mitchell-Hedges of Canada, all the others, each differing somewhat in size and detail, are held in museums or private collections. There is one in the Museum of Mankind in London, another in the Trocadero Museum in Paris; yet another has disappeared into an unknown location in Mexico.

Carl and Jo Ann are both friendly, accessible people, easy to talk with, although very protective of their priceless possession.

"All of the skulls were originally found in Mayan ruins in Mexico and Central America," Jo Ann explained. "Max was found in a Mayan tomb at a site in Guatemala. All the skulls are very rare, each carved out of one huge piece of crystal. It has been estimated that Max came from a fifty- to sixty-pound piece that was over a half a million years old."

Jo Ann pointed out that Max had been carved "against the grain" of the mineral, in spite of the fact that quartz crystal is not

porous and very hard, thus making it difficult to carve. "In Max's case, with his *many* major inclusions, it would have been easy to crack or shatter him," she said. "Literally, Max should not exist."

Carl and Jo Ann listen with great interest to those men and women who claim that being in Max's proximity provokes images and visions within them. "Whether you believe any of that or not, if you simply look at the artifact on a scientific and archaeological level, you cannot help being overwhelmed and awed at the skilled worksmanship that was involved in creating him," Jo Ann told us.

"I often wonder if we can ever truly guess how Max was created or *when* and by *whom*," she continued. "It would seem that the ancient Mayans did not have the technical skills to have created these crystal skulls. Actually, they didn't have any metal tools of any kind, and there are no crystal mines near any Mayan sites. Yet it is apparent that they used the skulls in certain of their ceremonies."

What is known, Jo Ann said eloquently, "is that this very special artifact, buried for centuries amidst the ruins of a once-flourishing civilization, has found its way back into the world of today. Max is the symbol of an unknown legacy from a mysterious and ancient past."

The Crystal Skull of Texas is the only such artifact in the United States available for public display. From time to time at special gatherings, Carl and Jo Ann permit audiences to touch Max singly and to have their own special experiences, feelings, and visions inspired by the skull's mystique. Private time with Max, by appointment only, can be arranged.

"The people who meditate upon Max always seem to get messages or feelings; and they often see visions of some sort within the crystal that they are able to apply to their own lives," Jo Ann said. "They see scenes from the past history of Earth, and very frequently they perceive UFO-related scenes and messages. While I do not understand *why* this occurs, it would seem that Max is much more than a rock. Everyone seems uplifted and happy after spending time with Max."

# CHAPTER TWENTY-EIGHT

# SEDONA—THE SOUTHWEST'S MOST MYSTICAL CITY

The other-worldly beauty of Sedona, Arizona, would in itself immediately qualify the area as being enchanting. The unique aspects of nature's handiwork that have shaped the majestic red rocks were fashioned over millions of years as the region was first covered by ocean, then desert, then ocean again, and now high desert country. Visiting Sedona, located about 120 miles north of Phoenix, allows the traveler to literally transport himself from a modern metropolis to an almost surreal wonderland in the matter of a few hours.

Those visitors who have perceived the red rock country surrounding Sedona with their normal senses have declared it to be one of the most awe-inspiring and beautiful places on Earth. Likewise, the *sixth* sense of the paranormally talented has hailed the area as one of the most mystical places on the planet.

For years, many metaphysicians have maintained that there is a spiritual city which exists in another dimension directly above Sedona. According to these seers, the ethereal city focuses energy down on the area.

Sedona has become a kind of pilgrimage region for at least the last fourteen years. Metaphysical leaders regularly hold major seminars near the vortexes, those mysterious areas of electromagnetic anomalous energy.

Many New Age teachers believe that the Sedona area retains powerful energies from the ancient American Indian or pre-Amerindian civilizations and that these forces exert a great influence on contemporary psychic-sensitives. Since both of the authors of this book are deeply involved in UFO research as well as the practice of American Indian Medicine Power, our experiences near the vortexes have been empowering and enriching.

In July of 1987, we visited a Medicine Wheel at one of the vortexes as an aspect of a Vision Quest seminar that we conducted under the sponsorship of Dr. Patricia Rochelle Diegel and her husband Jon Terrance. It was at that spot that our friend, author and publisher Timothy Green Beckley, noticed that Sherry had slipped away from the group and had moved out on a ledge to meditate. Not wishing to disturb her, Beckley walked quietly behind her so that he might take some photographs of her during meditation. As Sherry went deeper into the meditative state, he was able to photograph a most remarkable occurrence.

Sherry has practiced extremely deep meditation for many years, and we have both observed that she often attracts powerful energy fields about her body. As she sat meditating at the vortex, Beckley was able to photograph electromagnetic energies moving toward her. The energy field grew stronger and stronger, until, to the camera's lens, her physical body had all but completely disappeared—and Sherry seemed to have become totally at-one with beautiful, harmonious vibrations of light.

"Living in Sedona is like living in the fourth dimension," said Del Mary, an internationally acclaimed artist who moved to the area from Hawaii. "It is almost as if I died and didn't know it and I am living in this other realm, a step beyond all other places I know.

"And when you walk in these lovely hills," she continued, "it is almost like walking with the Masters and with Jesus. This may sound strange to those who have never visited here, but there is a feeling here that the ego goes—and you just feel one with everything."

In 1987, Eva-Grace Chicorel left the hectic environment of New York publishing for the "heaven" of Sedona. "I have a feeling of great connectedness here," she explained. "No matter what I do, it's right. I feel that not only am I in the flow, but I feel that all the people that I meet, I have known somehow before. I feel totally amongst friends."

Clarifying a common misconception among certain outsiders that Sedona has become a haven for cultist activity, Eva-Grace said that the people with whom she is acquainted are not into cults, but rather their own growth. "The people here accept each person for *who* they are and *where* they are on the kind of path that they chose for themselves. This process is called 'tolerance,' and it is so rare nowadays."

Eva-Grace has been delighted to discover a tolerance for all life forms in Sedona. "It is so easy to communicate with animals here— and they with you. I've always liked animals, and here even the wild animals simply seem to participate in my life."

Charmaine Yarune Boericke, a Los Angeles transplant, said that she often felt in Sedona as if she were walking with one foot in earthbound reality and the other foot in another dimension. "I never know exactly just which side I'm on," she laughed, "but it is all magic and it is all so beautiful."

Charmaine pointed out that the natural beauty of the place simply had to add to its mystical dimension. "One thing that particularly affects me is the wonderful colors here," she said. "The red rocks reflecting the brilliant blue sky is absolutely overwhelming."

Charmaine is completing a book on nature spirits, and she told us that she had seen quite a number of the etheric entities in the Sedona area. "I have found them to be quite different from the ones I have met before in other places. I don't always see elementals. I wish I could. Nor can I tell you how to see them. It is just when I'm particularly filled with an exquisite joy and love that they just suddenly appear...and they are as solid as you are.

"The energies that I have found in Sedona," Charmaine continued her explanation of the distinctive differences among elementals, "are very strong—and sometimes quite capricious. I have been
knocked off my feet. A few weeks ago, I turned a somersault in the
air and landed on my face but I did not hurt myself. At first I
couldn't believe what had happened, and then I realized that it had
been a friendly thing, and that the entity had taken care of me so
that I would not be hurt. I could have been badly injured because I
was walking on rocks going downhill."

Ardie Nicholls had been an accountant and bookkeeper for various firms and businesses in Phoenix for many years before she
moved to Sedona to open her own practice. That was six years ago.
Today she manages the Crystal Castle, a metaphysical bookstore
and gift shop.

"In the words of Patricia-Rochelle Diegel, one of the nation's
most esteemed ladies of the paranormal, Sedona is 'Shangri-La
West,'" Ardie said. "And there are times in winter, fall, and spring
when the clouds come down or when it is foggy and you look up
at these red mountains and you feel that you are in Shangri-La.
And even though you may read the newspaper and watch television and listen to the radio, somehow the rest of the world seems
very far removed from you here in Sedona. It's like we're sealed off
from the rest of the planet—and all of its troubles just can't quite
get through to us."

Patricia-Rochelle Diegel moved to Sedona from Hawaii in 1982,
and she stated that it had taken her over twenty years to earn the
right to settle in her "Shangri-La West." Today, she and her husband, Jon Terrance Diegel, live in a beautiful home on an acre of
land with "all kinds of elementals" running around the strawberry
patch and the rosebushes.

"My intuitive abilities have increased a thousandfold since we've
moved here," she said. "I feel that we have a real 'Mecca' here, like
no other place on Earth."

Mary Reagan is an astrologer and Reiki practitioner who moved to Sedona from Los Angeles five years ago. Rooted in her craft, she didn't expect any "funny" stuff to happen to her.

"After I had lived in Sedona about two years, I went with a group to Bell Rock for a 'toning' experience," Mary said. "The leader told us to put our hands on Bell Rock. He said that we were to close our eyes and go into the rock.

"I was thinking to myself, because I am a very analytical triple Virgo, 'Now wait a minute, I need about three days to research this first.'

"Then the leader told us that nothing was correct or incorrect. It will all be as it is supposed to be. So I expected nothing.

"He continued with the directive that when we put ourselves into the rock, our guide would be there for us. And all of a sudden, I'm *inside* the rock. It's like a cave. It's all red inside. And there are all these Indians with loincloths. My guide was right there on my left side.

"All of a sudden," Mary stated, "I *know* that I am one of those Indians...as well as this person standing observing them...as well as the person outside leaning against Bell Rock.

"That was the beginning of my being able to have dreams at night where I know that I am the one in bed having the dream, but I am also aware of being in the dream and of being outside watching the whole dream scenario take place. I know that this is leading toward some profound illumination experience—and I know that these kinds of experiences are common in Sedona."

Karen Webb, who manages a radio station in Florida, does not reside in Sedona, but, as a frequent visitor, it is her fervent hope that one day she will be able to call the area her home.

"I seem to blend with the energy here and become one with it," Karen said. "I am more in tune with a much higher frequency when I am here. I have had some most unusual experiences in Sedona, and I expect that I will continue to have more. I know that

I will accomplish a significant transformation in my life while I am in Sedona."

For Jo Tinsley, a Wiccan, Sedona is the perfect environment for a practicing witch. "This area is so gorgeous, and it is absolutely perfect for studying plant life, trees, animals—and all those things that most witches are brought up on.

"The minute I first came up here and saw those red rocks, I said, 'I'm home!' And I'm going to stay, because I am the crone, the old one. I'm doing more studying and reading than I ever have. I think Sedona opened up my brain somehow."

The author of *The Sedona Vortex Experience*, Gaia Johansen Lamb guides visitors on outdoor journeys to experience the much-touted vortexes of the area. "People undergo healings, personal transformations, the opening of energy centers—just marvelous, marvelous experiences," she said.

A vortex seems to be an area of some kind of unidentified electromagnetic phenomenon that certain people claim aids them in meditation, inspiration, and revelation. UFOs, ancient Atlantean super science, Indian spirits, and ethereal inhabitants of other dimensions have also been suggested as the origin of the vortexes.

Gaia's own introduction to Sedona occurred in 1980 when she was driving through the area, unaware that such a place even existed. "I pulled into the Chapel of the Holy Cross and had a mystical experience there," she stated. "The next morning I looked at the red, red rocks and the blue, blue sky—and something inside me just opened up. I went home and told my life partner, Maury, that I think we ought to move to Sedona."

"Home" for the Lambs had been in Sacramento, California, where Maury was a highly successful practicing psychotherapist. Maury had been on a spiritual path for several years and he was sensitive to his wife's mystical experience in Sedona, but his work in Sacramento was expanding at an incredible rate. Would he be

able to make a living in a town of around seven thousand population?

"I asked my own guidance," Maury told us, "and it came very clear to me that I was to move to Sedona. It was the first time that I had ever felt the energy of a place. I had previously been very aware of energy from people, but not energy from a place. It connected with me so profoundly."

Maury and Gaia found Sedona to be at once the most wonderful—and the most painful—of places in which they had ever lived. "It is a combination of the agony and the ecstasy," he stated. "But each offering of pain has given me a gift of knowing myself in a more intimate fashion. And each gift of self-knowing has allowed me to touch other people in a way that I never could have before.

"What I've seen here in Sedona," he emphasized, "is that the people who are truly committed to the spiritual path are also the ones that feel the agony. Part of my role is to help them touch the ecstasy. That's been part of the magic of Sedona for me."

Keith Alexes Boericke was a landscape artist in Berkeley, California, a man in a highly responsible, high-pressure position, spending over seven million dollars in seven years to beautify the city environment. "I burned out," he said frankly. "And I got fed up with California."

It was while he and his life-partner Charmaine were seeking counsel from Patricia-Rochelle Diegel that they both got hooked on Sedona. Comfortable now in his work as a healer with a special interest in vibrational medicine, Keith stated that he has seen practitioners in Sedona do "incredible things," both with instrumentation and their own minds. "I have witnessed occurrences here in Sedona that I never dreamed I would ever see!"

In Keith's opinion, a great majority of those living in Sedona today are re-expressing an Atlantean time period. "I think that we were a part of the period in Atlantis when the technology, the mental gymnastics, the wizardry, and some of the magicianship was strong; and it is strong again at this time. I believe that being in

Sedona has put us closer in contact with the cell memory of the Akashic Records of the Altantean consciousness.

"Those of us who are living in Sedona—whether we are conscious of it or not—are coming closer to the Akashic Record vibration of recapturing some of the techniques and impressions that were part of the period of advanced technologies on Atlantis."

Keith went on to inform us that although his academic background was in land management and landscaping, he had begun to invent certain instrumentation which he felt would be extremely useful in various healing techniques. "If one can properly focus the energy here in Sedona, it can truly assist one in truly remarkable creations," he said. "The problem is that the energy here is so intense, it can hit the lower chakras of our body. It can hit sexuality. It can hit emotionality. But if a person can establish a focus and the necessary discipline, he can tap into a higher consciousness. Sedona offers you the opportunity to tap into some wonderful energies—but it does take discipline!"

Prior to his move to the area, Keith, as an expert on land management, had never put much stock in the stories that he had heard about the various energy vortexes in Sedona. "Now," he stated firmly, "I believe that the whole area is an energy vortex!"

Jon Terrance Diegel agreed with Keith's observation that the whole of the area serves as some kind of remarkable energy vortex.

"I must be perfectly honest," he said candidly. "I was not as enthusiastic as my wife Patricia was about moving here. I had no love for the desert. I have always lived near the ocean, in California or Hawaii. I thought moving to Sedona would be like moving to a valley on the Moon.

"And it seemed as though everyone was raving about the energy at one of the many alleged vortex sites," Jon went on. "I had been to all the vortexes, and I had never felt a thing at any one of them.

"But then a strange thing happened to me. After we had moved to this place without an ocean—but with all the things that I thought I wouldn't like—I found that I didn't want to leave. When

Patricia and I would go out on lecture tours, I found that after four days away from Sedona, I wanted to go home. After we had lived here two and a half years, I didn't even want to drive to Phoenix, which I had loved very much!

"So what is it about Sedona that makes people not want to leave?" Jon put forth the question for his own earnest consideration as well as ours. "It is very difficult to explain. I guess in my case, I feel very safe here. Now I must immediately add that I don't feel safe *from* something. It is not that when I go outside of Sedona I don't feel safe. It is just that *this* is where I feel very, very comfortable.

"That is why I now feel that the entire area of Sedona is a vortex of energy," he said. "You can tell just about where that energy kind of shifts. It is not as clear-cut as knowing an exact spot on the map where it shifts. It is more subtle than that. But at certain perimeters of the Sedona area, you just feel secure and safe. It is like you have come home, and you've closed the doors behind you."

Gwen Monique Richland was a mental health care professional in New Mexico and later had her own metaphysical center in Las Cruces. She had heard a great deal about Sedona, but her initial visit there had resulted in a very bad personal experience. She had decided that the mystical city was simply not her cup of cosmic tea.

"But then I went to Albuquerque to hear one Patricia-Rochelle Diegel lecture," Gwen said. "Later, I got a reading from her, and she turned my life around about a hundred eighty degrees. I have been working with her or for her ever since.

"I have traveled extensively," she added. "In Sedona I have found something that is unlike anything that I have seen or known anywhere in the world. There is an energy here that is both demanding and rewarding.

"I have now resided in Sedona for a little over three years. The first two years were really rough going. I think Sedona tries you, really tries you to the hilt. You either stick it out, or Sedona will spit you out. I'm stubborn Taurus. I'm sticking it out!"

171

❖

Lydia Smithers is a marine scientist who specializes in working with dolphins. While she was serving as a midwife to a pregnant dolphin in Florida, Lydia underwent a mystical experience during which she saw herself in the water, surrounded by dolphins, in a place with a turquoise sky and red cliffs. She was so impressed with the vision that she later painted what she had perceived in the trancelike state. A friend told her that she had depicted a scene in Sedona, Arizona, an area completely unknown to Lydia.

"When I got to Sedona and saw the Chapel of the Holy Cross, I realized that that was what I had painted," Lydia told us. "The strong impression that I had then was 'Okay, now I have come home!'"

"The planet Earth is not a familiar planet to me," Lydia said. "In fact, there have been a lot of times when I said, 'Father, why did I ever say I could go there? Why did I ever think I could make a difference?'

"I arrived in Sedona, and I felt home for the first time in this life experience. I had the impression that this was where I had been seeded into human form on Earth."

Lydia, as do so many others in Sedona we interviewed, stressed the "multidimensionality" of the area. "This was very confusing for me in my first year living here, because I would see the past, the present, and the future simultaneously. I would get very frustrated because I could not get *inside* those red rocks—and I knew what was inside. I could not get to the temples, to the Light Beings. I could see them, but I could not get this third-dimensional form there. I could get there in spirit, but not in the body."

Lydia also emphasized the sacredness of Sedona. "The Indians say that God put his hand on Sedona, and I think that is what I truly feel about Sedona, as well.

"Everything is accelerated here," she said. "The learning process is intensified. You absolutely cannot hide here. If you have made a spiritual commitment, it comes true here. I think you get about fifty lifetimes in the matter of a few years when you live in Sedona.

Sedona is my mystery school—the past, present, and the future—
and it is my home!"

# CHAPTER TWENTY-NINE

# Sky Beings and the Gathering of Eagles

Jon Terrance Diegel remembers vividly the night in 1954 when, after a college dance in Orange County, California, he and his date decided to crawl out on the large rocks that enter the ocean near Balboa.

"It must have been about one-thirty in the morning," Jon said, "and we sat watching the lights of the little boats that were fishing in the canal. It was an extremely picturesque and romantic scene, and we decided to continue all the way on the rocks to the very end of the jetty.

"We were about halfway there when I looked up at the sky because I heard something that sounded kind of like the wind," Jon recalled. "Coming from the land side and going toward the ocean was a craft that was every bit as large as a 747 jet—or larger. But, of course, we had no jet aircraft like that then. The commercial airlines still used propeller planes. This thing picked up speed as it went, and it was over the horizon in about twelve seconds. It didn't make any mechanical-type sounds. There was only the sound of the wind moving past it."

Searching his memory further, Jon recalled that the UFO definitely had "portholes, which were lighted." He could discern no wings or tail on the craft.

"It was long, so I'd have to say that it was cigar-shaped. It was

very low and only about fifty yards away. Needless to say, it scared the beans out of us, and we went home immediately!"

✛

The remarkable enigma that is known as the UFO mystery manifests itself all over the Southwest, but some observers of the phenomenon state that one can almost guarantee a sighting in the skies over Sedona, Arizona.

Eva-Grace Chicorel said that she wished to preface her account of her UFO experiences by establishing that she is by nature a very skeptical, show-me kind of person who for many years was a publisher of reference books in New York City. She first visited Sedona during the much-publicized Harmonic Convergence in August 1987, and she somehow found herself with a group of people looking up at the sky and, heeding the dictates of their group leader, sending messages of love to the UFOnauts.

"All of a sudden, we saw lights in the sky that zigzagged and performed manuevers that no airplane could have accomplished," she said. "By the end of the evening, not only did I know that UFOs existed, but so did a very skeptical scientist who was in our group."

Eva-Grace has now lived in Sedona for four years, and she has become accustomed to sighting strange lights in the sky. But just a week before we interviewed her in September 1991, she had undergone a most remarkable experience.

During the morning, Eva-Grace told us, she had been in her office, doing her usual "very grounded, mundane kind of work." But around noon, she had become so tired that she felt she could no longer sit up. She felt that she had no choice but to go to her bedroom and lie down.

"The moment I did," she said, "I saw a man standing at the end of my bedroom, but there were no walls visible. He was of average height and he wore an unusual kind of three-piece suit. His eyes were slightly slanted, and he looked at me with friendliness. I felt no fear of him.

"Then, suddenly, there were all kinds of little 'people' all around

175

him," Eva-Grace continued her account. "I couldn't see them clearly, but I knew that they were about half his size. Then I felt this pain on both sides of my groin, and I knew that *they* were doing *something*. I tried various ways of extracting the pain from myself, of drawing it out. But *nothing* worked.

"Then it occurred to me that maybe these entities were not from the Light, but may have come from the dark side, so I asked the one that looked like a human being, 'Are you from the Light?' There was no answer."

Trained in the Huna techniques of the Polynesian traditional priests, Eva-Grace immediately performed a "kind of exorcism." She firmly stated that if there were any entities "within, around, below, or above" her who were not of the Light, they were to leave her at once.

"It is not like me to command," she said, "but this time I did, and I asked that Divine Light fill the spaces that the entities had occupied. I made this command twice, and I felt the pain leaving my groin. It went slowly down and out of my body—and disappeared.

"Discussing the experience later with some friends, we came to the conclusion that because of the other work that I was doing, the whole episode could have been some kind of test," she concluded.

Famed artist Del Mary told us that she was brought up on UFO literature, but after years of scanning the night skies for a glimpse of an unidentified glowing, zig-zagging object, she had never had a sighting of any kind.

"I had friends and various acquaintances sometimes point to the sky and say, 'Look there! There's a ship, there's a UFO!' And I would say, 'Uh, huh,' because I would only see stars twinkling or pulsating," she said.

When Del Mary moved to Sedona some years ago, she thought for certain that she would soon have a dramatic UFO sighting.

Sedona was, after all, the place to see UFOs, right?

"After living here for *eight years*, I still had not had any kind of UFO sighting," she laughed. "Then, one night, I was sitting on the

deck of our house with my husband Rick, and off near Schnebly Hill, there were seven huge stars that looked like the Big Dipper. The trouble was, it was in the wrong place to be the Big Dipper.

"Rick ran in the house to get his binoculars, and we saw that there really were seven ships, seven UFOs, moving over the airport vortex. They were luminous and round—and they were not stars!

"Those seven went by, and another seven came after them," Del Mary said. "It was absolutely incredible. And then Rick yelled, 'Sweetheart, look! Another seven!' And all of them just went 'way off, and you could hear this hum in the sky. Rick and I just stood there with this wonderful feeling of love."

Del Mary recalled that the remarkable incident had occurred around ten-thirty in the evening and that after the UFOs had left, the entire sky had glowed pink. "There was only a quarter-moon that came up over Schnebly Hill. There wasn't enough light from that to light up the whole sky like that. We just felt total love and bliss coming from the ships."

✤

Patricia-Rochelle Diegel has given over forty-eight thousand past-life readings, and, according to her meticulous files and her remarkable memory, a good many of those men and women have experienced prior existences on other worlds and in other dimensions of reality.

"I have several notebooks full of descriptions of what my clients looked like when they first came to Earth in their alien bodies— and this includes the Lizard People," she told us.

"I have determined that there were certain reasons why the people who had extraterrestrial past lives came down to the planet Earth," she went on, explaining her findings. "It seems as though the main underlying purpose was to speed up the evolution of the slowly evolving Earthlings, who had just come out of caves.

"From time to time over the past several million years, actual extraterrestrial entities have come to Earth to bring us certain types of culture and creative thoughts and to develop scientific methods when the Earthlings were ready for them. A lot of these ETs liked it

so well here that they became addicted to Earth and didn't want to go home when it was time for their ship to leave. These particular entities got 'stuck' here.

"Even though their extraterrestrial bodies appeared to be immortal compared to the Earthlings' bodies," Patricia-Rochelle said, "they did eventually die. And since there were no extraterrestrial bodies for their spirits to inhabit, they had to come into human bodies and begin an evolutionary path going back up the ladder.

"I feel that so many of us who remember that we are from someplace else, got very emotional when we saw the movie *ET*. When ET points up to the stars and says, 'H-O-M-E,' I wanted to cry—because I have felt that way ever since I was a little girl."

In addition to establishing a magnificent reputation as a painter of extraordinary talent, Luis Romero feels that his special mission is to help his brothers and sisters awaken to the memories of their extraterrestrial heritage.

"Some people have felt so misdirected in life because they have not remembered or realized that they were ETs until we got together and talked about it," Luis said. "Then they found out a lot about themselves."

Luis and his wife Jean visited Sedona for several years before they finally moved to the mystical city. "I always felt so alive here," he said. "It was as if I had come back home. And the longer that we have been here, the closer that Jean and I have become.

"It seems as though the energy here either draws people closer together or pulls them apart. We have had so many UFO sightings since we've been here. There are always four or five 'ships' over Sedona. Our work here revolves around the 'space people' and Jean's mystical prose."

Professionally, of course, Luis finds that living in Sedona has been of great value to his painting. "I get inspiration by simply looking out the windows at the red rocks. There is a certain energy that comes from them that enables me to go back in time, to remember the past and a time when I am certain that I was here before."

Jean Romero emphasized a caution that must be observed by those coming to Sedona to experience UFOs and any other mystical manifestations.

"Because of the high energies of the place, everything is intensified here," she said. "If you tend toward anger, you might experience greater anger than you've ever had. If you tend to be happy, you'll probably experience a higher and a greater happiness. Those red-rock energies magnify whatever one is or feels. It is imperative to develop discernment about these energies. This kind of environment teaches you some discipline in order to be able to live here."

Jean suffered severe "catastrophic illnesses" in the past year. "If I had not been in this particular place," she said, "I can't imagine that I would have had the beautiful healing experiences of my body, mind, and spirit. But in Sedona there is such a concentration of healing energies and people who work with those energies that I was able to contact the people I needed to, as well as my own spirit help, so that I got over some pretty dire circumstances in my physical being."

We asked Luis to explain about the Gathering of the Eagles, the UFO meetings the Romeros sponsor from time to time in Sedona.

"Many people feel that they are strangers here on Earth, and they don't identify with or relate to much of what the majority of humankind focuses upon," he said. "Meeting others who have similar beliefs gives great strength and a clearer sense of mission and purpose.

"The Gathering of the Eagles is the bringing together of those of extraterrestrial consciousness in this area, and it is a way of making connection with each other," he explained. "It is also a gathering of all the clan to manifest the love aspect that is needed on this planet. It is really, simply put, a way to help these people to express their love and to carry that love to all they meet."

Luis' source tells him that love is the key, the glue that holds the universe together. "We on Earth need to develop love so that the extraterrestrials can come and do the work that they need to do to help us put the planet back to what it should be."

The Romeros have sponsored four gatherings thus far, one a year

since they received the inspiration to put out the call for those of extraterrestrial awareness to come together for clan meetings.

Jean and Luis told us that in the beginning they were guided simply to place an ad in the paper that said no more than "A Gathering of Eagles," a date, and a place. Nothing was said about what the meeting's purpose would be.

"And yet," Luis said, "when the time came, the hall was packed!"

On faith, the Romeros had obtained a certain number of imitation eagle feathers which they were told they should pass out to each person who attended the gathering. As Jean and Luis faced the unexpectedly large group assembled before them, they realized that there were four or five times more people than they had feathers.

"But I just kept reaching into the basket and pulling out another feather to give to someone," Luis said. "It became like the miracle story of the loaves and the fishes in the New Testament. The feathers just kept multiplying like magic until each person had been given a feather. Miracles *do* happen!"

# CHAPTER THIRTY

# GHOSTS GALORE IN OLD SAN DIEGO

The thing that strikes you as you walk the reconstructed streets of Old San Diego is that the place actually looks and feels haunted. Many of the original buildings date from 1846. The earliest Mexican adobe dwelling was constructed in 1827. The sense of history is as powerful as the quickening of the sixth sense that tells you that you are not alone when you enter some of the old homes and business places.

Old San Diego is the birthplace of California. On Presidio Hill, Father Junipero Serra established the mission of San Diego de Alcala on July 16, 1769. In the early 1820s, a small Mexican community was formed that by 1835 had evolved to El Pueblo San Diego. The first U.S. flag was raised on Old San Diego's tree-lined plaza in 1846. Because it was the site of the first permanent Spanish settlement on the California coast, San Diego is as significant to the Pacific heritage of the United States as is Jamestown, the first English settlement in Virginia Colony, to our Atlantic ancestry.

When we visited Old San Diego in September 1991 we headed first for the Robinson–Rose house, a structure that had been built in 1853. Constructed to contain both a family home and numerous stores and offices, it was the first commercial building in San Diego. Today, the house serves as the state park visitor center.

On our way we passed El Fandango Restaurant, which accord-

ing to old records, was built over the original site of the Machado family home. The Machados were influential members of the community, and there are two remaining mansions that bear their name.

A waiter named Marcos arrived at El Fandango a bit after four o'clock one morning to begin preparations for the 8:00 A.M. breakfast crowd. He remembered that it was a cold and damp morning, and as he walked through the main dining room to turn on the lights, he saw a woman in white sitting at the far corner of the room.

As he attempted to identify the woman, he noticed that she seemed to have a cloudlike, hazy appearance. Realizing that he might be perceiving an apparition, Marcos ran to turn on a light. As is so often the case in such ghostly encounters, the sudden light apparently caused the phantom woman to vanish.

At first reluctant to disclose any details about his paranormal experience, Marcos was finally persuaded by his wife to mention the sighting to others.

Soon after word spread of the waiter's strange guest, two historians of the area not only took Marcos seriously, but also pointed out that in the early and mid-1800s, many of the Machado women would have worked at the precise spot where he had seen the ghostly figure.

According to Jack and Faye Brussel, writing in the *Old Town Gazette* for September 1991, research is now in progress "with a highly accepted historian, a Machado descendant herself, digging into the past in an attempt to identify our 'Lady at the table.' An artist is working with Marcos to document, on canvas, what our lady looked like."

✛

When we visited the old Catholic cemetery, where so many prominent figures of Old San Diego are buried, we met the genial and courteous Father Lazarus, who, in jeans and tee-shirt, was industriously digging in the hallowed ground. An accomplished historian, he explained to us with a broad smile that he had that

very day discovered a previously unknown grave. He was in the process of erecting a marker to dignify the final resting place of an anonymous resident of Old San Diego.

As we stood amidst the gravestones of gunfighters, leaders of rebellions, and innocent babes, Father Lazarus told us of strange poltergeist disturbances that had afflicted a business place adjoining the old cemetery, which is now in the heart of Old San Diego's commercial area.

"You see, this old cemetery originally stretched down the street where those businesses now stand and out into the middle of what is now Old Town Avenue," he said. "The poltergeist kept interfering with many of the electrical appliances, the alarm system, and so forth. The haunting just keeps coming and going there."

By far the most haunted place in Old San Diego is the Whaley house, constructed in 1857. Here the ghosts do not "come and go," they remain on the premises and seem to be eternally active. Indeed, the Thomas Whaley mansion, completely furnished with authentic antiques of early California, may be among the most haunted houses in the United States.

June Reading, the amicable and knowledgeable director of the Whaley house, told us that immediately after its completion, the mansion had become the center of business, government, and social affairs in Old San Diego. The oldest brick house in Southern California, the mansion served as a courthouse, a courtroom, a theater, and a boarding house—as well as the family home of Thomas and Anna Whaley and their children.

The remarkable clairvoyant Kay Sterner had earlier told us of the time when the Research Committee of the California Parapsychology Foundation had been called upon by the San Diego Historical Shrine Foundation to investigate the hauntings in the Whaley house. Footsteps had been heard in the master bedroom and on the stairs. Windows, even when fastened down with three four-inch bolts on each side, would fly open of their own volition—often in the middle of the night, triggering the burglar

alarm. Screams had echoed throughout the upstairs, and a large, heavy china closet had tipped over by itself.

Responding to June Reading's request, Kay Sterner, a former educator and a psychic sensitive of well-established reputation, agreed to give her impressions of the old house. Prior to her first visit, Mrs. Sterner knew absolutely nothing about the Whaley family or the history of the mansion in Old San Diego.

Before she entered the house, the clairvoyant picked up the image of a scaffold and a hanging man on the south side of the mansion. Mrs. Reading corroborated the impression by stating that ten years before Thomas Whaley had constructed his home, a sailor called Yankee Jim Robinson was hanged on the site of what would later become the arch between the music room and the living room. Thomas Whaley had been an observer when Yankee Jim kept his appointment with the hangman.

Next Mrs. Sterner saw a gaudily dressed woman with a painted face lean out of a second-story window. June Reading felt that the ghost may have been that of one of the theatrical troupe that had leased the second floor in November 1868.

Seconds later, Mrs. Sterner saw a lady in a mauve gown lean far out the window and stare down at her. On a later visit, the clairvoyant pointed out the same gown on a mannequin in one of the bedrooms. Mrs. Reading identified the lavender lady as one of the Whaley daughters, both of whom were excellent seamstresses.

The Court House Wing of the mansion revealed impressions of "rowdy, rough characters and seafaring men." The Court House is generally thought to be the most haunted spot in the Whaley house, due to the violent emotions that were expended there in those early days in Old San Diego.

Sitting alone in the dark in the upstairs hall, Kay Sterner saw clearly the disturbing image of a young woman engaged in abortive suicide attempts. Later, a stocky man wearing boots and carrying a logbook in his hand came toward the psychic sensitive. He appeared to be an attorney upset about a case in progress, and he walked with a noticeable limp.

Mrs. Reading verified the suicide of a young woman who once

lived in the house. The woman, apparently of unsound mind, made several attempts before she successfully accomplished the morbid deed.

The description of the man matched that of Squire A. R. Ensworth, Thomas Whaley's lawyer and business manager, who was also a magistrate. Ensworth had broken his leg in a fall on the property, and it had never been correctly set.

On another occasion, an older, well-dressed woman passed by the clairvoyant on the stairs without noticing her. "The woman was dressed in a dark, greyish-purple gown and bonnet," reads the report in Kay Sterner's book, *A Psychic Explores the Unseen World.* "She passed so close [Kay Sterner] could see the fine crimping on her bonnet...the extremely fine hand-tucking...the texture and color of the material of the blouse. The woman carried a lighted candle in a little tin chamberstick, with one finger, as if checking the house for the night."

June Reading said that other sensitive visitors to the Whaley house have also perceived the image of Anna Whaley, who still watches over the mansion she loved so much—and who deeply resents the intrusion of strangers.

In 1964, Mrs. Reading related, the television talk show host Regis Philbin and his friend saw Anna Whaley as they sat on the Andrew Jackson sofa at 2:30 A.M. "The 'image' floated from the study, through the music room, and into the parlor. At that moment, Philbin, in nervous excitement, dissolved the apparition with the beam of his flashlight. Since that time, night visits have not been permitted."

In addition to the sightings of the primary spirits of Thomas and Anna Whaley, Mrs. Reading said that the other ghosts most often seen include Yankee Jim Robinson, who walks across the upstairs sitting room to the top of the stairs; a girl named Washburn, who was a playmate of the Whaley children; and "Dolly Varden," the family's favorite dog.

And then, of course, there are the screams, the giggles, the rattling doorknobs, the cooking odors, the smell of Thomas Whaley's favorite Havana cigars, Anna's sweet-scented perfume, the sound

of footsteps throughout the house, and the music box and piano that play by themselves.

Nor must we forget the many visitors to the Whaley house who have heard the sounds of a crowded courtroom in session and the noisy meetings of men in Thomas' upstairs study.

There are ghosts galore in Old San Diego.

# CHAPTER THIRTY-ONE

# INDIAN SPIRITS THAT WALK CITY STREETS BY NIGHT

"I knew that I should never have let Rudy buy that old Indian skull that someone made into an ashtray," a very distraught Ethel Onslager of Edmond, Oklahoma, told us. "I know that is what set that Indian's spirit on us."

According to Ethel, her husband had bought the grim curio from a man at a roadside stand outside Tulsa. "The fellow that sold it so cheaply to Rudy seemed awfully anxious to get rid of it," she recalled. "Now I understand why. I argued against Rudy's buying it from the get-go. I said it was tasteless, vulgar. Who'd want that ugly, grinning thing setting on his desk or anywhere else? Besides, I told him that it didn't seem right, since those old Indians were human beings, too."

Rudy is an accountant who does a lot of paperwork at home. The first night that he set the skull ashtray on his desk, he came back after dinner to find important sheets of figures scattered throughout his office. He blamed it on a freak draft of some sort.

And then his computer started acting up. It just didn't do what he told it to do. And one time when he was working late on a set of important statistics for a local oil company, the computer blinked twice and erased every bit of input that he had just spent eight hours inserting.

"The capper for us came the night about a week after he had

bought the skull when Rudy started screaming that his office was on fire," Ethel said. "I came running in with a fire extinguisher and papers were burning every which way. I blamed the fire on his godawful smoking habit, but Rudy swore that he had been careful to put out every cigarette in his grotesque ashtray."

Later that same evening when they were watching an old Randolph Scott Western on the late show, Rudy and Ethel both felt a prickling sensation on the backs of their necks.

"We turned around at the same time to see this Indian in full regalia standing beside the desk in Rudy's office," Ethel stated. "He didn't say anything. He just scowled and pointed at the skull ashtray on Rudy's desk. Then he disappeared."

Rudy, who had never even believed in Santa Claus or the Tooth Fairy as a child, sat up wide-eyed all night. "The next morning, he couldn't get rid of that ashtray fast enough," Ethel concluded. "He told me he just tossed into a city dump! And once he did, his office—and our lives—returned to normal."

Since the late 1960s, men and women in increasing numbers throughout the Southwest and the entire United States have reported the appearance of American Indian ghosts. Some theorize that the manifestation of such entities reflects the guilt that the collective unconscious of the United States may be experiencing as a more sensitive and aware nation comes to grips with the often cruel and callous manner in which the various tribes were dealt with during the periods of the Indian wars and the westward expansion. Certainly such popular motion pictures as *Dances with Wolves, A Man Called Horse,* and *Little Big Man* have served the dual purpose of presenting the aboriginal tribespeople as having been much more than animalistic savages and of depicting in graphically explicit drama how savage were the white men in betraying the spirit and the substance of their treaties with the red men.

In the "California Living" section of the Los Angeles *Herald Examiner* for October 13, 1968, Wanda Sue Parrott stated that the bulk of ghost reports received by the *Herald Examiner* at that time

had to do with the manifestation of American Indians.

In one of the cases, a woman identified as Mrs. W. was told by the ghost of an Indian man that he would leave her apartment only if she disposed of the Indian artifact that she had recently purchased. Mrs. W. did as the specter bade her, and even though the ghost was true to its word and left along with the artifact, she was so unnerved by the eerie encounter that she sought the counsel of a psychiatrist.

To her amazement, the doctor consoled her with the admonition that there was nothing wrong with her. Many of his patients had undergone similar experiences with the ghosts of American Indians.

Ms. Parrott also recounted her research, which indicated that a number of San Gabriel Valley residents had also shared in the "Indian ghost experience." Men, women, and children alike, she wrote, had all reported seeing Indian ghosts appear in their yards, bedrooms, and living rooms at all hours of the day and night.

Some years ago we spoke to a woman whose family had recently constructed a home in the immediate proximity of an Indian burial ground. For obvious reasons, the woman requested anonymity of both name and location, but her account was quite impressive, powerfully emphasizing just how thin the line can become between the living and the dead.

The family, whom we'll call the Andrews, learned that their house had been constructed on sacred ground; here many Indians had been massacred and piled into a mass burial site. Almost immediately upon moving into their new home, the Andrews experienced poltergeistic manifestations and the unnerving sight of spirit forms projecting themselves about the house.

"Our home often receives violent slams at night, and we can often hear drums beating," Mrs. Andrews told us. "Other people, even nonbelievers in this kind of thing, have heard the drums and seen the spirit forms.

"When the Moon is full—especially in August, September, and

189

October—you are more apt to hear the drums," she explained, "although we certainly are not devoid of them at other times. On some nights you can see what looks like masses of Indians carrying torches. They seem to be gathering for some kind of ceremony."

❖

It is always best to stay away from sacred ground when you are building houses or constructing highways. Our friend Don Red Fox told us of a road crew that plowed through sacred burial grounds in Oklahoma with a sensitivity as cold and indifferent as their bulldozer blades.

"When they unearthed skulls and bones, some of the workers dressed up the grandfathers and grandmothers in old clothes and made scarecrows out of them," Don said. "One guy, a trucker, who hauled gravel to the construction site, put sunglasses on a skull and put it in a cab with him as his 'second driver.'"

Not long after such desecration the workers began to suffer a series of accidents with the expensive machinery breaking down that were at first annoying and costly but progressed to a number of close calls that were life-threatening.

"By the time that a group of us traditional tribespeople arrived with a medicine priest, the men were ready to listen to us," Don said. "Several of the workers who had been on the site after dark had seen things that they could not explain, so these sightings, plus the series of accidents, convinced them that they should give us back the bones of our grandparents and permit us to rebury them in new ground that the priest had made sacred."

For many years Don Red Fox, as representative of a committee of traditional Native Americans, traveled throughout the United States seeking to persuade museums, curio shops, and private collectors to surrender the skeletal remains of the grandparents on display so that they might be returned to their respective tribes for sacred reburial.

"We have no interest in collecting the arrowheads, pottery, and beadwork from the museums, the shops, and the collectors," Don told us. "We have no more interest in these artifacts than any

American who might be curious about the history of this country, and we have no intention of establishing our own museums stocked with such objects. We only wish to rebury the skeletal remains that are languishing in Anglo museums and to provide the grandparents with sacred interment in consecrated ground. We feel this is no different from, let us say, a Roman Catholic who might not wish to see his grandparents' bones on display and who would desire to see that they were buried in consecrated, holy, ground."

On more than one occasion, according to Don Red Fox, curio shops or museums who denied his peaceful request suffered a series of mysterious fires in the area in which the bones of the tribal grandparents had been showcased.

"By all that I hold holy, I swear that neither I nor any human agency was responsible for these fires," Don insisted. "It was the energy of the Great Mystery seeking to soften the hard hearts of the curators and the shopkeepers. In a number of cases, I received calls from those who had at first refused my request, who were now asking me to come back to remove the skeletons."

✤

"I thought that I had acquired a thing of great beauty in the old Hopi wedding basket that I bought in Flagstaff, Arizona," Karla Scheinberg told us. "I had no idea at that time that there were disreputable opportunists called pothunters who violated Indian burial sites and looted them for their artifacts. I understand now that there is big business in authentic Native American artifacts and that there are international rings of these graverobbers."

In her new apartment in Scottsdale, Karla centered the Hopi basket above her fireplace mantel, giving it a place of honor among her bowling trophies, family pictures, and the spelling champ award she had won in fourth grade back in Minnesota.

That night she watched David Letterman until after the Viewer Mail segment, then went to bed.

"The next morning, I was both puzzled and disturbed to find that the fireplace mantel had been swept clean," Karla said. "All my family pictures, the trophies, all the knickknacks were dumped

on the floor. The Hopi wedding basket was laying across the room. I have no pets, no cat to jump up on the mantel and scatter things.

"I got really frightened thinking that some pervert had somehow got in and vandalized my apartment while I slept. I thought of all the horror films that I had seen where some psycho terrorizes the heroine before he assaults her or murders her. You never think anything like that will happen to you."

Karla was nearly hysterical when she awakened the next morning to find that someone or something had once again unceremoniously dumped everything from her fireplace mantel on to the floor.

"That night I asked my boyfriend to stay with me and to sit up to see if we could catch whoever—whatever—was messing up my apartment and my mind," Karla said. "I must admit that about three in the morning we kind of forgot about trespassers and slashers and were creating a much more pleasant scenario in my bedroom. That was when our lovemaking was interrupted by the sound of someone crying."

Karla and her boyfriend cautiously walked out to her living room and were shocked to see the hazy form of an Indian woman dressed in traditional garb seated before the fireplace. At first her back was to them, but the woman seemed to sense their intrusion into her sorrow, and she turned to look at them.

"Her eyes were swollen and red from crying," Karla stated, "but then she gave us a look of fierce anger. She pointed at the wedding basket, and I swear that I heard a voice inside my head saying, *'Give it back to me!'*"

Seconds later, the apparition vanished.

"My boyfriend always likes to pretend that he is so macho and so masculine-logical, but he was really pretty badly shaken by the experience," Karla stated. "The next morning we drove up to Flagstaff, and we just continued driving around the area until I felt a special kind of feeling. Then I threw the basket out the window. I don't know if we did the absolutely right thing, but the ghost hasn't come back to mess up my apartment."

✛

Those attuned to the ways of traditional Indian medicine hear such accounts of American Indian ghosts and recall the prophetic warning of Chief Seathe (Seattle) to the white men who cheated his people out of their lands with the Treaty of Point Elliott in 1855:

"Every part of this country is sacred to my people. Every hillside, every valley, every plain and grove has been hallowed by some fond memory or some sad experience....

"When the last red man shall have perished from the earth and his memory among the white men shall have become a myth, these shores will swarm with the invisible dead of my tribe....

"At night when the streets of your cities and villages shall be silent, and you think them deserted, they will throng with the returning hosts that once filled and still love this beautiful land.

"The white man will never be alone. Let him be just and deal kindly with my people, for the dead are not altogether powerless. Dead, did I say? There is no death, only a change of worlds."

# CHAPTER THIRTY-TWO

# THE RETURN OF THE THUNDER BEINGS AND AMERICAN INDIAN PROPHECIES OF COMING EARTH CHANGES

**W**e would like to conclude this book of strange, unusual, and supernatural occurrences in the American Southwest with a chapter of great importance and far-reaching implications for the entire world.

Few people would argue that the 1990s are a time of great transition, and while certain political walls are being torn down, old barriers of prejudice and hatred are too often being maintained with renewed vigor. The drums of war, while perhaps muffled at the present time, can too quickly sound again if ancient, smoldering coals of anger should be fanned into raging fires of destruction.

In such troubled times of stress and apprehension, many people turn to the Bible to seek out prophecies of a new world and its promise of a better existence. While some interpret such biblical revelations to speak of a currently popular philosophy concerning a "new world order," others feel the apostolic predictions warn against specific events of a highly negative nature that will occur should a new world order come to pass.

While some people find both comfort and admonitions in biblical prophecies, others ponder the warnings of the American Indian medicine priests of the various tribes that foresee a time of Great Cleansing, a process of purification to be endured by the Earth Mother and by those men and women who will survive a terrible

series of catastrophes. What is more, these wise ones refer to their ancient traditions which state that our planet has undergone cycles of death and rebirth, destruction and reconstruction.

Each of the American Indian tribes with which we are familiar repeats legends that tell of their people emerging from the destruction that had been visited upon a former civilization. The majority of these accounts deal with the surviving people having escaped from a terrible flood, which immediately suggests both the biblical story of the Deluge and the tales of Atlantis.

The Navajos say that their ancestors escaped the terrible flood through a long, hollow reed. When they reached safety, they were taken in spirit through space to visit other worlds, the Moon, the stars. After the waters had subsided on Earth, they returned to live on the mountains and in the cliffs. They preach that the world will again be destroyed if humankind cannot control its wickedness.

The Arkansas Indians tell of a destructive flood that was sent to Earth from the Great Mystery because of humankind's propensity to waywardness. The more pious survivors made their way to the North American continent in order to remain separate from others who might again become corrupt.

The Mandan Indians believe that their ancestors rode out the flood in a big canoe, which came to rest on a mountain when the waters subsided.

The Yuchi tribe tells of a big flood that drowned all but those who had been warned of the impending disaster. After the flood, the survivors attempted to build a high tower in which to take refuge should such a deluge again strike Earth. (The accounts of the Mandan and the Yuchi are highly reminiscent of the biblical accounts of Noah, the Ark, and the Tower of Babel.)

The Delaware recount the story of a continuing struggle between the humans of Earth and the Snake People. Resolving to destroy humankind, the Snake People brought about a great rushing of water to drown all humans. A female spirit helped some men to a boat and saw them to safety. The immigrants landed first in a cold country, but gradually worked their way to a more temperate land.

The Seneca Legend of the Seven Worlds says that the world of

humankind has relived the traumatic experiences of birth, death, and rebirth six times before and that all of humanity now stands on the brink of destruction prior to entering the final world in our evolutionary cycle.

The Hopi agree and say that we are about to enter the final world after a last great war, a war that will be "a spiritual conflict with material matters. Material matters will be destroyed by spiritual beings who will remain to create one world and one nation under one power, that of the Creator."

The Hopi's Armageddon pitting spiritual against material forces will occur when the "Saquasohuh [Blue Star] Kachina"—now represented by a faraway, yet visible blue star—makes its appearance. The process of emergence into the final world, however, has already begun.

For the American Indian traditionalist, the destructions of the previous worlds have all been a necessary part of humankind's spiritual evolution. Easily distracted humans forget the lessons of the Great Mystery and fall away to rely upon their own feeble devices. When this state of affairs comes to pass, the Great Mystery causes a time of Great Purification, which cleanses the Earth Mother for a new epoch, a new world.

The Amerindian prophets are not alone in their catastrophic theory of history; the holy books and legends of many peoples recount tales of war between the heaven and the earth. Cosmic revolutions and civil wars were said to have rent the prehistoric worlds on several occasions. More than one Sodom and Gomorrah exploded so that "the smoke rose up like that from a mighty furnace."

In each of the ancient legends of previous civilizations being decimated we read of governments rendered impotent, commerce abandoned, cultural attributes forgotten, once-mighty cities crumbled to rubble. But always a remnant of people survive.

Enough human seed is retained to perpetuate the stubborn and surviving species. The cycle of the death and rebirth of civilization is maintained. Humankind returns to the primitive to relearn the basics, to recall the essentials. It is as if humankind must continue to replicate the progression of hunter to farmer to merchant to scientist

to philosopher until we get it right and graduate from ape to angel.

The great medicine people are all saying that another time of purification has rolled around on the great cosmic calendar. We are about to enter a time of earthquakes, vulcanism, and dramatic earth changes. The Amerindian prophets tell us that we can do no more to prevent the cataclysms before us than we can to prevent the advent of winter. But just as a knowledge of the past reminds us that, regardless of our fears, winter will come, it also informs us that we can prepare for the bad times. In like manner we can begin to make preparations for the Great Purification and to plan ahead for the planetary springtime that awaits those members of humankind who endure.

The late Dallas Chief Eagle of the Teton Sioux once clarified that from the view of Amerindian theology there is no such thing as the "end of the world." There is fast-approaching a time of colossal upheavals, he emphasized, but no death of the Earth Mother.

Hopi traditionalists are storing food and water for the coming Great Purification. Their Medicine Priests have told them to expect a terrible famine. Canned and dehydrated foods, seed, kerosene lamps, bottled water, and water purification tablets are being put aside in carefully concealed caches.

The great medicine prophet Sun Bear has told us that his tribe is judiciously putting away stores of food and survival materials in the manner of the Hopi. He reminded us that one of the ancient prophecies states that the Great Purification will come after the white man builds a house in the sky. "We believe that prophecy referred to Skylab, so we have long seen signs that the cleansing has begun," he said.

Don Wanatee of the Mesquakie (Fox) tribe foresees what will possibly be a great fire of some kind that will "rearrange things" on the planet. "The great catastrophe will leave pockets of men and women who will begin to people the Earth again," he said.

Wanatee does not wish to be counted as a doomsayer, but he feels that the time of great catastrophe is near. "I am one who believes in the prophecies of the Mesquakie," he stated. "They prophesied great trailways in the sky. They said that the animals

197

would be dying. They said when many species would become extinct, humankind would begin to see unusual things. There would be floods, earthquakes. It would be as if the Earth were revolting against its inhumane treatment."

As we indicated in the preceding chapter, many medicine priests also predict that we will see more and more Indian ghosts walking the land.

"These ghosts are coming back to touch the white man's heart. They are coming back not only for the Indian's sake, but for the sake of the entire globe," said Dallas Chief Eagle.

"We traditional people are the guardians, the living, visible keepers, of the Earth Mother," Sun Bear said. "The ghosts are the keepers and protectors over us."

Sun Bear issued a caution that although there are currently guardian forces all over the land, there are also spirits of destruction hovering about us. "You can see the expression of the energies that they have created," he said. "These destroyers will soon unleash their entire strength. The only people who will retain their balance will be the people who have linked into their minds the things that are really solid and true. These people will survive because they will keep themselves away from the centers of strife and destruction."

Over the past thirty years, the great Shoshone–Cherokee medicine priest Rolling Thunder, who now lives outside Carlin, Nevada, has been looking for those balanced men and women whom he calls the Thunder People. It will be the Thunder People who will be on a level of awareness high enough to assist others during the coming times of planetary purification.

Thunder, he explained, in the ancient mythologies of Scandinavia, Greece, and the Amerindian, means "telling the truth." Rolling Thunder is seeking out those who can put their minds together as one "to believe in truth, justice, and peace."

Rolling Thunder suffers pain of the spirit over all the violence that permeates the land and the destruction that is visited upon the

Earth Mother. "Thunder People will seek to straighten things out in peaceful ways," he said. "If enough people prefer peace, there will be peace. If the next war is allowed to happen, there will be no winners. If one of us suffers, we are all going to suffer."

✦

Page Bryant, a nationally recognized psychic, teacher, and lecturer who has only recently moved from Sedona, Arizona, to the Southeast, has become extremely involved with Medicine Ways. For a time she was closely allied with Sun Bear and spoke at many of the Bear Tribe's Medicine Wheel Gatherings. In a series of visions, Page was shown the seven chakras (energy centers) of the Earth Mother.

"The base chakra, the kundalini of the Earth, is located in the Pacific Ocean, and is known as the 'ring of fire,'" she stated. "This is the opening in the etheric body of the planet that allows the 'fire of Spirit' to permeate the planet and therefore raise its consciousness. As the Earth Mother evolves—she is magnetic and feminine—the 'ring of fire' area will provide the energy for evolution and spiritual growth."

Page said that she was told by her Source that the Solar Plexus of the Earth Mother, a magnetic chakra, is in the area covered by the central part of the Atlantic Ocean.

"The spleen chakra is in the area of Alaska, the northernmost United States, and western and northernmost Canada, as well as the fringes of Siberia," she said. "This is the chakra that deals with cleansing and purification. These are clean and pure lands, touched only by those who are in balance with the Earth."

Page was shown in one vision that the heart chakra of the Earth is located in the area of the United States known as the Four Corners, a place where the states of New Mexico, Arizona, Colorado, and Utah are joined together. "The joining forms the ancient symbol of the equal-armed cross," she stated, "a symbol of nature and of manifestation. The heart center is the love center of the planet. This center, which represents brotherhood, is situated on Indian land."

In another vision, it was revealed that the throat chakra of the Earth Mother was to be found in the area of land mass that we call Puerto Rico, another magnetic center. "We think of the throat as the tool of communication and speech," Page observed, "therefore it is interesting to note that this area is the physical home [at Arecibo] of the largest radio telescope in the world—a scientific tool that serves as an offer of communication to the vast reaches of the universe."

The brow center of the planet was shown by her Source to be in the area of Tibet, Mongolia, and China. "Through the civilizations that have developed in these lands and through the efforts of Mother Earth herself, the spiritual eye has been, and still is, in the process of development," Page commented.

The crown chakra, according to Page's revealed information, is located in the center of the Gobi Desert. "While this area is a vaste wasteland," she admitted, "it is also the site of the energies of Shamballa and the divine energies of the entire sphere."

Page Bryant has stated that it is an important part of her quest to learn how the Amerindians learned to live so well on the Earth Mother. "I give thanks to the Great Spirit that there are a few of the Indian wise ones who are coming forward during this preparation period for another initiation of the planet," she said. "I thank them for sharing their knowledge and for opening up the path to all humankind, so that we might share in this understanding of our Home."

Grandmother Twylah of the Seneca is one of the most revered of the medicine priests who are sharing their knowledge and their wisdom in this coming time of cleansing and initiation.

She foresees dramatic earth changes which will occur before the end of this century.

"The Thunder Beings are truth beings," she said, referring to the great cosmic entities that now gather for the coming time of transition. "Their teachings are of truth, and they are filled with love. In these final days, it is important to think of unconditional love and not to permit anything to interfere."

Grandmother Twylah believes that the Thunder Beings are now speaking to everyone, "but only the awakened Thunder People are listening." In order to hear the Thunder Beings, she gave firm advice: "Go within...go within...go within. Go within to your vital core."

With her greatly esteemed quiet eloquence, Grandmother Twylah told us that "long before time was born, love, truth, and peace were tiny, primordial seeds nestled within the vibral core of the Earth Mother. Love, truth, and peace were gifts of the Great Mystery, pristine emanations that would exist for time eternal.

"Truth embodies idealism," she went on. "Peace brings the harmony. Love supports truth as the primal sensitivity that bonds comfort between two or more entities, and peace is the outgrowth of harmony among all forms of life. Therefore, love provides the supportive energy for truth to achieve peace—within...within...within...the vibral core of all life forms. The Great Mystery, the source of all life, created every form of existence to be nestled within...within...within...as one body, one heart, one mind, one spirit."

Speaking of the future, Grandmother Twylah delineated that the year 1991 had been the year of challenge, but 1992 will be the year of change. Continuing on, she stated that 1993 will be the year of choice; 1994, the year of commitment.

"So people had better get on their horses and decide which direction they're going to be going, because by 1995, there will be so many changes that it won't make any difference how much they know," Grandmother Twylah said. "The important thing will be that they are able to stand in their truth. Those who stand in their truth will eat whatever Mother Nature provides—and it will be roots, bark, and seeds. Before this decade ends, we will be crawling on our bellies—but we will be surviving.

"The great fires have already begun," she stated. "The Middle East set the flames going. The earth is warming up, the ice is melting, so the land is going to go under. The Earth Mother is changing her garments. She's going to put on some new stuff. She is going to be dancing around. And it is about time! She's sick and tired of the way she's been treated."

201

Grandmother Twylah repeated the importance of standing in one's truth during the troubled times ahead. "Supposing right at this moment the earth began to quake and up in the sky world there would be thunder and lightning and so much noise that we couldn't think. The best thing that we could do for our survival would be to stand on our truth. To run in panic never accomplishes anything."

Mary Elizabeth Thunder is part Cheyenne, part Mohawk, part Irish, and adopted Lakota. In 1981, after spending many years of her life as a specialized counselor assisting those afflicted with dependencies upon alcohol and drugs, she suffered a heart attack and underwent an afterlife experience. During the process of her recovery from the trauma, certain of her Elders, such as Leonard Crow Dog, Wallace Black Elk, Grace Spotted Eagle, and Rolling Thunder, advised her to focus on her work as a teacher. Mary has followed the Sacred Pipe to Thunder-Horse Ranch outside of West Point, Texas, where she lives with her husband Jeff White Horse and conducts a wide range of workshops, seminars, sweats, and vision quests.

"Prophecies are given to us as possible outcomes if we don't wake up and participate in the change," Mary Thunder has said. "Seeds of a new consciousness are raining down on the planet, very much like the time when the human race was formed here on Earth millions of years ago. Now Mother Earth is pregnant again, and she is birthing a New Dimension—so we as a race have some twenty-five years or less to raise our consciousness to be in tune with the Oneness of Universal Truth. God is our image of what we are becoming. We have to take responsibility for how we envision our future of the planet as a whole."

Mary recalled the words of Rolling Thunder when he observed that all the pollution on Earth comes from the minds of men. "We must make our lives spiritual twenty-four hours a day," she said. "We must eat and drink natural foods. We must give up drugs and other poisons to our systems that only confuse, dull, and degenerate the mind and body."

In Mary Thunder's view, we are at the time of illumination for Planet Earth. "We have a message of love and peace for the revolution of spiritual consciousness in these last years before the great change. As a Sun Dancer, I bring a message of healing from the Sun behind the Sun. It is healing in a balanced way—male/female, positive/negative, Father Sun/Mother Earth. The Native Americans were always the ones with secrets of 'grounding' and of balancing opposing forces. We must return to the natural ways. We must heartfully learn that we are a part of All That Is. Mother Earth is within us, and we are within her. We *can* recognize ourselves as vehicles of the Great Mystery, and we can return to the original instructions of spiritual laws for guidance. We can learn to heal with the natural medicines of pure air, clean water, fertility, and solar rays."

On the summer solstice in 1988, representatives of the Incas, the Aztecs, and many North American tribes gathered in an agreed upon location to make the announcement of the dawning of a new era. In order to prosper in this time of rebirth, humankind must return to the natural way of living and remember the spiritual laws of old.

"Native Americans believe that all children—all of us—come from one father and one mother—Father Sun and Mother Earth— so we are all brothers and sisters," Mary Thunder said. "All blood is the same color, the color of living fire. All nations of the world from the beginning have had the same natural flag—the rainbow. Grandma used to say that we were like a bouquet of flowers—different colors, but all the same, beautiful in a bouquet.

"The heart of the Sun is open for all of us to heal ourselves and Mother Earth. The time for choice, for all of us, is right now. Pray for the people so the people might live."

We will end this book with such a prayer, a prayer that recognizes that we are members of one great body of humanity, each of us born for the good of the other; that we are one great planet, all beings bound together in oneness by the strength of the Great

Mystery; that we are one infinite, beloved universe, all powers and principalities bound together by unconditional love. If we stay ever vigilant against the Dark Side of the Force, then we shall forever share our mysteries and our love.

# About the Authors

**B**RAD STEIGER is the author of more than one hundred books with over fifteen million copies in print, ranging from biographies (*Valentino, Judy Garland, Jim Thorpe*); inspirational (*Revelation: The Divine Fire, The Healing Power of Love*); phenomenal (*Mysteries of Time and Space, Beyond Belief*); Native American (*Indian Medicine Power, Kahuna Magic*); and UFO research (*Project Bluebook, Strangers from the Skies, Star People*). In addition to the nonfiction works listed above, Steiger is the author of two novels and more than two hundred short stories, which have appeared in such magazines as *The Saint, Alfred Hitchcock's Mystery Magazine,* and *Fantastic.* In 1977, Steiger's *Valentino* was made into a motion picture starring Rudolf Nureyev. In that same year, he coscripted *Unknown Powers,* winner of the Film Advisory Board's Award of Excellence.

**S**HERRY HANSEN-STEIGER studied at the Lutheran School of Theology in Chicago, where she was later placed on staff. An ordained and licensed minister, she served as a counselor at SUNY (Stonybrook) and Smith Haven Ministries. Hansen-Steiger is also the cocreator of the highly acclaimed Celebrate Life Program and in 1972 established The Butterfly Center of Wholistic Education. In 1978, she was one of the founding members of the Wholistic Healing Board through the institutes of Health and Education, Washington, D.C. Additionally, Hansen-Steiger is the author of *Seasons of the Soul* and coauthor with her husband of *The Teaching Power of Dreams, Indian Wisdom and its Guiding Power,* and *Hollywood and the Supernatural* among others.